Routledge Revivals

Gold, Prices and Wages

First published in 1913, this *Routledge Revivals* title reissues J. A. Hobson's seminal analysis of the causal link between the rise in gold prices and the increase in wages and consumer buying power in the early years of the Twentieth Century. Contrary to the assertions of some notable contemporary economists and business-men, Hobson contended that the relationship between gold prices and wages (and the resulting social unrest across much of Europe) was in fact much more complex than initially supposed and that there were significantly more important factors in the rise of con-temporary wealth. In this work, Hobson considers the rapid enlargement of state enterprise and joint stock companies; a wide extension of banking and general financial apparatus; and the opening of profitable fields of investment for the development of underdeveloped countries, which helped raise the rate of interest and profits.

Gold, Prices and Wages

With an Examination of the Quantity Theory

J. A. Hobson

Routledge
Taylor & Francis Group

First published in 1913
by Methuen & Co. Ltd

This edition first published in 2010 by Routledge
2 Park Square, Milton Park, Abingdon, Oxon, OX14 4RN

Simultaneously published in the USA and Canada
by Routledge
270 Madison Avenue, New York, NY 10016

Routledge is an imprint of the Taylor & Francis Group, an informa business

Publisher's Note
The publisher has gone to great lengths to ensure the quality of this
reprint but points out that some imperfections in the original copies may
be apparent.

Disclaimer
The publisher has made every effort to trace copyright holders and
welcomes correspondence from those they have been unable to contact.

A Library of Congress record exists under LC Control Number: 1
13000111

ISBN 13: 978-0-415-58940-6 (hbk)
ISBN 13: 978-0-203-84468-7 (ebk)

ISBN 10: 0-415-58940-1 (hbk)
ISBN 10: 0-203-84468-8 (ebk)

GOLD, PRICES AND WAGES

GOLD, PRICES & WAGES

WITH AN EXAMINATION OF
THE QUANTITY THEORY

BY

J. A. HOBSON

WITH TWO DIAGRAMS

METHUEN & CO. LTD.
36 ESSEX STREET W.C.
LONDON

First Published in 1913

PREFACE

THE current rise of prices is an exceedingly attractive problem for two reasons. The first is its intellectual toughness and intricacy. For though a great deal has been said and written on price-movements during the last hundred years, it cannot be said that anyone has explained in a really satisfactory way why and how prices move.

The other attraction is the enormous practical importance of the problem. Never has this been clearer than at the present time. For whatever other causes contribute to the ' social unrest ' from which most nations are suffering, it seems certain that the rise of prices has acted everywhere as a main source of irritation.

Both these attractions led me to the inquiry which forms the subject of these chapters. It was not with the hope of reaching a complete

solution that I entered it. Nor do I claim to
have reached one. But the confident assertion
of some economists and business men that the
problem was in reality a quite simple one, the
rise of prices being evidently due to the enlarged
output of gold in recent years, had never seemed
satisfactory to me. I therefore decided to try
to work out the problem afresh, testing the chain
of causation connecting gold with prices, and
bringing under survey certain other industrial
and financial factors which seemed relevant to
the issue.

Accepting at the outset the self-evident proposition that a rise of prices means an increase
in the quantity of money paid for goods greater
than the increase in the quantity of goods, I
divided my inquiry into two sections. The first
section concerned itself with possible causes of
the acceleration of the supply of money : the
second with possible causes of the retardation
of the supply of goods. For a rise of prices may
evidently be brought about in either of these
two ways, or in both.

My investigation into the supply of money
confirms the view that an acceleration of pur-

chasing power is a large factor in the rise of prices.
But the acceleration of purchasing power is not
directly attributable to the increased output of
gold. The influence of gold, either as coin, or
as a support of credit, is much smaller than has
been represented. The great extension of bank
credit, which constitutes the acceleration of
supply of money, is primarily due to three causes.
Two of them relate to its supply, one to its
demand. The rapid enlargement of enterprises
in various countries, undertaken by states and
municipalities, and accompanied by an equally
rapid development of joint stock companies, has
enabled a largely increasing proportion of property to figure as security for bank credit. Along
with this movement has gone a wide extension
of banking and of general financial apparatus.
Thus there has been a great growth in those
forms of wealth which are the real basis of credit
and in the machinery which manufactures
credit. So much for the means of supply.

A great demand for credit has coincided with
this enlargement of the means of its supply.
The chief factor in the enlarged demand has been
the opening up of new large profitable fields of

b

investment for the development of new or backward countries, chiefly in America.   This demand
for developmental capital has raised the rate of
interest and profits, stimulated a full use of the
new potential supply of credit, and has been
a principal direct agent in the rise of prices.

The quite recent growth of facilities for credit
explains the acceleration of supply of money.
But since a large use of credit promotes industry, it might appear that the accelerated
supply of money should be attended by a
corresponding acceleration of supply of goods.
In such an event there could have been no rise
of prices.

An investigation into the industrial or goods
side of the problem shows, however, that the
growth of supply of goods, though doubtless
considerable, has been much slower than the
growth of credit.   This is explained partly by
the above-mentioned change of business structure, which has enlarged the proportion of existing wealth available as basis for credit.   But
other causes have directly assisted to retard
production, especially the vast unproductive
expenditure of modern states, the increasing

wastage involved in the competitive distribution of modern commerce, and last, but not least, the temporary stress which the new investment policy has laid upon those industrial operations throughout the world which conform to the so-called law of diminishing returns. When the full fruits of the development of South America and Canada are reaped, the acceleration of supply of goods may be found to balance or outweigh the further growth of the supply of credit, and prices may cease to rise, or even fall.

Meanwhile, the counterplay of these two sets of forces, the one expanding the production of credit, the other checking the production of goods, seems to give the best explanation of the current rise of prices. The part played by the enlarged output of gold is a useful though a minor one. It has facilitated the operation of the forces stimulating credit, by furnishing the larger gold reserves which, though to a diminishing extent, are still required to maintain the easy currency of credit-notes. It is a condition, but not a chief efficient cause of the acceleration of supply of credit.

In a concluding chapter I reconsider 'the quantity theory of money,' adducing reasons for holding that, when it passes beyond the status of a self-evident proposition, and asserts the determination of prices by gold supply, it is erroneous. Discussing the paradox of the divergence between the hire-price and the purchase-price of money, I urge as a solution the view that all forms of money in their circulation are hired instruments of the exchange of commodities, the passing holders of which pay a hire-price for the single service of exchange which they require, not being concerned with the actual value of the instrument employed.

Such are the principal conclusions to which the inquiry leads. Some of them seem tolerably certain, others tentative or dubious. I indicate them here in the preface in order that busy readers may make up their minds, before starting, whether it is worth while to follow a line of reasoning which introduces into the solution of the price problem so many considerations incapable of exact statistical measurement and, in some instances, highly speculative in their character and influence.

I desire, in conclusion, to express my deep indebtedness to Mr. F. W. Hirst and Sir George Paish for many valuable points of information and of criticism.

J. A. HOBSON

LONDON, *February* 1913

CONTENTS

DIAGRAMS

GOLD, PRICES AND WAGES

CHAPTER I

THE RISE OF PRICES

§ 1. AT the outset of an inquiry into the rise of prices it may be well to put on record a few leading and generally admitted facts.

From 1873 to 1895, a large and fairly continuous fall of wholesale and of retail prices took place in Great Britain.

From 1896 to the present time a considerable, though less regular, rise both of wholesale and of retail prices has taken place. The rate of increase has been faster since 1905. The rise in retail prices, as indicated by cost of foods, has been closely correspondent with the rise of wholesale prices.

From 1873, a year of high wages, until 1895, money wages made no considerable change. They fell considerably in the 'seventies, and rose considerably in the 'eighties, remaining pretty steady in the early 'nineties. From 1895 to the present time they have been rising. But this rise of money wages has failed to keep full pace with the rise of prices. Real wages have fallen since 1895. This fall has been more marked since 1905.

These price-changes are found in all other leading industrial countries. In the United States, Canada, Germany and France, the rise of prices has been greater than in this country. This is made evident by the following table, compiled by Mr. Hooker : [1]—

Average.	United Kingdom (Board of Trade).	United Kingdom. (Sauerbeck).	France (Réforme Economique).	Germany	U.S.A. (Bureau of Labour).	Canada (Department of Labour).
1890–1899 .	100	100	100	100	100	100
1900–1909 .	104	111	109	115	118	115
1910 . .	113	118	118	128	132	125
Sept. 1911 .	...	122	126	139	...	...

Retail prices, however, have risen in other countries at a somewhat slower rate than whole-sale.

The rise in prices of raw materials since 1895

[1] "The Course of Prices," *Journal of the Statistical Soc.*, Dec. 1911,

has been greater than that of foods in Great Britain, Germany and France, and considerably more violent in its variations. In the United States and Canada the two growths of prices have moved closely together, the prices of food rising equally with those of materials.

§ 2. The index figures which register these rises of prices relate entirely to certain raw materials and foods sold in wholesale markets. For those are the only classes of articles for which reliable prices are available. A theoretically complete index would, of course, take account of a great number of other objects of sale, manufactured articles, land, houses and other buildings, securities, professional and manual labour, etc., in a word, all sorts of goods and services on which money is spent. There are some who hold that, if all these prices were taken into due consideration, the general rise of prices would be a good deal less than our index figures suggest. Indeed, it seems likely that some reduction would be effected. For so far as statistics are available, the rise in the prices of fully manufactured goods is smaller than of raw materials. The price of old securities at fixed interest has largely fallen. The price of manual labour in most countries has risen less than the price of foods and materials. How far the rise of city rents is a higher price for the same article, or for a better article, we have no means of precise determination, though the increase of land values and the higher price of building materials and labour would seem to imply a not inconsiderable actual rise of price.

Where frequent changes in size, quality and other conditions of the article take place, or where great local variations occur, it is virtually impossible to apply the index number method. But these deficiencies do not invalidate our index numbers as much as may appear at first sight. For the chief materials and foods are genuinely, if not perfectly, representative. Important in themselves as marketable objects, they enter as main ingredients into most of those further or final commodities, the price fluctuations of which are not capable of register.

Though, therefore, the actual rise of general prices may be somewhat less than the index figures indicate, there is no reason to question the statement that since about 1895 a decided upward movement of world-prices has taken place.

§ 3. Now, more or less coincident with this general rise of prices, several other important changes, affecting the general course of commerce or finance, are observable. The most conspicuous of these has been the rapid enlargement of the world output of gold since the early 'nineties,

GOLD PRODUCTION OF THE WORLD SINCE 1851

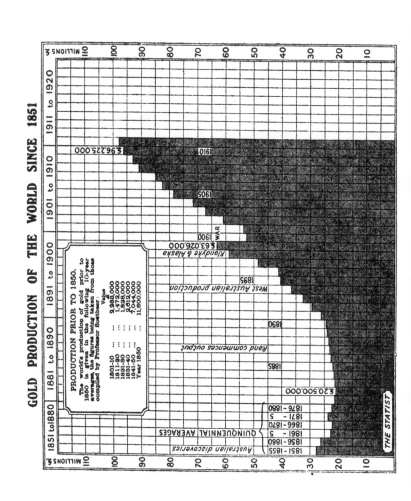

PRODUCTION PRIOR TO 1850.

The world's production of gold prior to 1850 is given in the following 10-year averages, the figures being taken from those compiled by Professor Soetbeer:—

	Value
1801-10	2,288,000
1811-20	1,472,000
1821-30	1,808,000
1831-40	2,012,000
1841-50	7,044,000
Year 1850	11,600,000

£96,275,000 — 1910

£63,026,000 — 1900

Klondyke & Alaska

1905

1900 WAR

West Australian production

1895

Rand commences output

1890

1885

£20,500,000

QUINQUENNIAL AVERAGES	
1876 - 1880	
1871 - 5	
1866 - 1870	
1861 - 5	
1856 - 1860	
1851 - 1855	

Australian discoveries

THE STATIST

MILLIONS £ 110 100 90 80 70 60 50 40 30 20 10

due in large measure to the discovery of the deep levels in the Transvaal and to the successful application of the cyanide process.

The rate of the enlargement in world output may be indicated by the following figures : [1]—

Year.						Annual Average.
1885–1890	.	.	.	.	.	£22,583,000
1891–1895	.	.	.	.	.	33,454,000
1896–1900	.	.	.	.	.	52,871,000
1901	.	.	.	.	.	53,629,000
1902	.	.	.	.	.	60,974,000
1903	.	.	.	.	.	67,337,000
1904	.	.	.	.	.	71,380,000
1905	.	.	.	.	.	78,143,000
1906	.	.	.	.	.	82,707,000
1907	.	.	.	.	.	84,857,000
1908	.	.	.	.	.	91,030,000
1909	.	.	.	.	.	93,376,000
1910	.	.	.	.	.	96,225,000
1911	.	.	.	.	.	97,448,000

The production for the period 1906-11 is described as " not far from being as large as the total stock of gold in various forms in Europe and America at the close of 1848."

§ 4. Along with this an exceedingly rapid growth of bank deposits in various countries of the world attests the growing economy of the use of coins and the extension of the machinery of credit.

In England and Wales the aggregate of

[1] United States Mint Estimates to 1911.

bank deposits grew steadily from the sum of £408,878,000 in 1890 to £776,650,000 in 1910. In Germany and the United States the proportionate increase has been far larger. The deposits and current accounts in German Joint-Stock Banks are given as £75,449,654 in 1890 and as £353,367,853 in 1907. In the United States, deposits in National and other banks grew from $591,900,000 in 1890 to $2,545,500,000 in 1909.

A recent estimate of the Director of the Mint in Washington indicates that the aggregate of bank credit in the shape of loans and discounts for the banks of the world has nearly trebled in the period 1889–1910.[1]

Associated with this extension of money and of the machinery of finance are certain important changes in the structure of businesses and in the application of industrial energy. An increasing proportion of the industrial and commercial business of the world is passing into the form of joint-stock companies. In the United Kingdom the paid-up capital of registered companies nearly doubled in the twelve years 1896-1908. In the United States the movement has been even faster, and in every country where capitalistic methods of production and commerce are well established, a similar structural change is taking

[1] *Report of the Director of the Mint*, p. 59.

place. An important effect and object of this change has been to increase very largely the proportion of the wealth of these countries available as a basis of financial operations, and in particular as securities for bank credit.

§ 5. Synchronous and connected with this development of joint-stock enterprise has been a very great enlargement of the area of profitable investment. The enormous migration to the United States, with the rapid expansion of its mines and manufactures, has been accompanied by financial operations on an enormous scale. The rapid and assured prosperity of Canada, following the realization of the agricultural resources of the North-West, has coincided with a continuous demand for capital on the part of the states of Central and South America. The rapid increase in the amount and the proportion of European, and especially of British savings, which has been flowing into these and other foreign countries for investment, must be regarded as factors likely to exert important influences, direct and indirect, upon the flow of money and the course of prices.

CHAPTER II

§ 1. THE statement that a general rise of prices has taken place this year means that the quantity of money paid for goods has increased faster than the quantity of goods. This, at any rate, is true of a world in which it is agreed that both quantity of money and quantity of goods are increasing all the time. An inquiry into the causes of a rise of prices involves, therefore, inquiring into the factors which regulate the respective rates of the increase of money and of goods. For a general rise of prices may be attributed to an acceleration of the growth of money or to a retardation of the growth of goods, or to a combination of the two processes.

But first let us be clear what we mean by quantity of money and quantity of goods. By money we mean anything which has a general purchasing power, by goods anything that is purchasable. But a statement of the number and denomination of the coins and notes, and of the size of the bank deposits upon which cheques may be **drawn** at a particular time affords no information about the quantity of money in its bearing upon prices. Similarly, a statement of the number of the various commodities and services which constitute the stock of purchasable things at a particular time sheds no light upon quantity of goods for the purpose of price-change.

§ 2. By quantity of money, regarded as a factor in price-change, we signify the amount of purchasing power actually applied in buying goods during a period of time, for example, a year. By quantity of goods we signify the quantity of sales of material articles and services actually made during that period. The same money-forms may be used many times in buying goods during the year. The same articles or services, changed or unchanged in their shape or nature, may be sold many times during the same year.

In the case of money this obvious truth is generally indicated by saying that money = currency and deposits multiplied by their respective velocity, *i.e.* the number of times they change hands in one year. In the case of goods which figure several times in processes of purchase, for example, as raw materials, semi- and fully manufactured articles, wholesale and retail merchandise, they are counted according to the quantity of 'transactions' which they represent. Some econo-

mists have preferred to keep a narrower significa-
tion of ' money ' and ' goods,' and to express the
price-equation in terms of ' purchasing power '
and ' transactions.'

But, seeing that the substance of each act of
purchase is the exchange of a sum of money for a
sum of goods, it seems better to retain the simpler
words ' money ' and ' goods '[1] for the general
terms of our price-equation, in preference to the
longer, vaguer ones.

§ 3. But, before opening out our investigation
into the increased proportion of money to goods
which constitutes our problem, we must examine
a little more closely what is meant by quantity
of money, and what determines how great the
quantity of money shall be.   To tell the number
of coins and notes in use and the rapidity with
which they move, and the quantity of cheques
drawn in proportion to the average deposits, is
merely a descriptive account of quantity of money,
and of business habits.   What we require to know,
primarily, is the causes which determine quantity of
money.   When we ask where does the money come
from with which persons buy goods, to tell us that
it comes from gold mines or from banks, is not the

---

[1] The term ' goods ' will be used throughout this work to
cover all sorts of things sold for money, whether raw materials,
finished material commodities, services or securities.

sort of answer needed at this stage. The persons who buy goods normally or regularly get the money with which they buy them by selling other goods. In a word, the ordinary source of money is the money previously received for goods sold. But where, we shall be asked, did that money come from ? From other payments made for other goods previously sold. In a word, setting aside for the moment the separate question of how the different forms of money came into existence and circulation, the quantity of money applied at any time to buying goods has been got by previously selling goods. If we could take the books of all traders and other persons engaged in selling anything, goods or services, the aggregate of their gross receipts or gross incomes would appear to constitute 'the quantity of money' for our price-equation.

§ 4. The importance of this approach towards 'quantity of money' is, that it gets rid at the outset of a mischievous assumption that the origins of money are quite independent of goods, and that the quantity of money may, therefore, naturally be expected to vary with no relation to the variations of goods.

Now, recognizing that the normal direct source of money at any time is payments for goods, it will rightly be presumed that the quantity of money should have a close relation to the quantity of goods.

And so it has. Most changes in the quantity of money are directly connected with and proceed from changes in the quantity of goods or transactions.

If a tradesman or other business man finds that the amount of money coming into his possession is greater than it was, the first and most natural explanation is that he is selling more goods than he sold before.

If the wheat supply of a market passes through the hands of a new class of merchants or importers, whereas formerly it passed straight from the exporter to the miller, the new set of transactions would presumably add as much to the goods side as to the money side of the equation. If a country, hitherto outside the commercial world, for example, a province of China, should come into it, its entrance into the world markets would increase the aggregate of money just as much as it increased the aggregate of goods. Previously, its supply of goods and of money used in the buying and selling of them lay outside the area of world-commerce, now they are both brought in and they may be assumed to add as much to the one side of the price-equation as the other.[1]

[1] This, of course, is only a general truth, requiring qualification. If a country with a previous low-level of prices comes

If all money were thus derived from prior acts of sale, the aggregate receipts rising and falling with the expansion or shrinkage of those acts of sale, it would appear as if quantity of money must vary directly and proportionately with quantity of goods, and that therefore prices must remain stable. And this would be true of an industrial community, either fixed in population and in its standards of production and consumption, or growing in such a way that it did not shift the proportion of its demand for different classes of goods. The only way in which prices could change, in a community where money was entirely derived from previous receipts, would be by a change in the direction of purchases. If a larger proportion of money were directed to buying goods whose production conformed to the so-called law of diminishing returns, the result would be a reduction of aggregate goods as compared with money, and therefore a general rise of prices. Conversely, an increasing application of money to purchase of goods, conforming in their production to the so-called law of increasing returns, would involve a general fall of prices.

In such communities it would be necessary

into the world markets, it will add more to the quantity of goods than to the quantity of money.

to look for the explanation of every change of prices to some alteration in the nature of consumption, and so of demand.

§ 5. But though the main and normal source of quantity of money is the payments made for goods previously sold, *i.e.* gross receipts, this is not the sole source. The quantity of money may be reinforced from outside sources.

There appear to be two other ways in which purchasing power can come into being. Though most gold coins are received in payment for goods sold, some are not. These represent fresh gold dug out of the ground and coined and stamped as legal tender by governments for the miners, who can take it, or its paper equivalents, and buy goods with it, just as if they had received it as payment for other goods which they had sold.

This is an addition to the volume of purchasing power which has no equivalent on the goods side. £1,000,000 of this new gold means so much new purchasing power, and no more new goods. Indeed, it would normally [1] mean a reduction in the supply of goods. For the £1,000,000 of new gold will have been got by withdrawing some capital and labour from other

---

[1] Unless it be regarded as a new 'rich find' involving no more use of capital and labour in gold-mining than before.

industries in which they would have produced a quantity of goods.

New gold, then, so far as it is used as purchasing power, forms an addition to the quantity of money derived from payments for goods sold.

§6. A second, and even more important supplementary source of 'money' is new bank-credit.

We must be careful to distinguish the nature of this addition to the money which constitutes gross receipts. When business men pay in to their bank account the coins, notes or cheques, received in payment for the goods or services they sell, the bank 'credits' them with the amount. But this 'credit' adds nothing to the aggregate quantity of money, though it enables buying and selling to be carried on more conveniently than if the 'money' were kept in the safes of the different businesses. It is only a convenient way of keeping the money belonging to the various business men who are buying or selling to one another.

In tracing the sources of money we must separate from the credit which thus represents money paid in to the accounts of customers out of their own resources, the credit which represents advances or other loans made by bankers. The bank deposits of a community at any given time are comprised partly by one, partly by the other sort of credit. But, whereas the former has never constituted an addition to the stock of money got from payments for goods, the latter has. When the banker first loaned it, placing it to the deposit account of his customer,[1] it operated as a creation of new purchasing power. He who received the credit found himself in possession of so much more ' money,' and no one had any less than before. Of course, as soon as this specially created money has once been expended, it begins to appear in the gross receipts of the businesses producing the goods on which it has been expended, and passes into bank accounts on ordinary terms with other cheques. What effect this bank-made credit has upon prices is, of course, exhausted by its first use by the borrower who uses it to supplement *ab extra* his ordinary supply of money got from selling goods. The person who next receives it in payment for

[1] For convenience we here treat the banker as the sole manufacturer of this credit. But, as we shall recognize in a later chapter when we consider more closely the production of credit, the banker only converts into a final monetary form the ' securities ' which are the financial shadow or representative of the ' investments ' which the saving classes have made, using stockbrokers and finance-houses as their agents. Out of the financial material of these securities and a certain amount of gold or other legal tender held by him as a ' reserve ' the banker fashions and loans this credit.

goods which the borrower buys, gets it not as an addition, but as an ordinary part of the gross earnings of his business. When first expended by the borrower it increases the aggregate supply of ' money ' in relation to goods and raises the level of prices. The level of prices once raised, it continues to assist the former amount of trade to be carried on at the higher level, but in its further ' circulation ' produces no further effect on prices.

If, then, we are analysing the supply of money during any given period, it is only the increase of credit during that period, not the aggregate of credit, that concerns us. An addition to the volume of credit affects the aggregate volume of money in just the same way as a new influx of gold, or of notes founded upon gold.

In understanding the relation of quantity of money to prices, this separation of the part of bank deposits paid in by customers from that advanced or loaned by bankers is absolutely vital. For to begin the analysis of money, as is often done, by regarding as fundamental the distinction between coins and notes in circulation on the one hand, and bank deposits on the other, is to preclude the possibility of any satisfactory solution.[1] It is, of course, true that at any given time the monetary forms in use can be divided into outside currency and bank deposits. But that distinction throws no light upon the question what determines the aggregate quantity of purchasing power paid for goods during the year. The really radical distinction is between the money received in payment for goods, some of which is paid into bank deposits, some not, and the money not received in payment for goods but coming

[1] It may be true, for instance, as Professor Irving Fisher argues, that a ' more or less definite ' quantitative relation exists between the volume of coins and notes in circulation (' money ' is his use of the term) and the volume of deposits. But such a relation, if it exists, seems quite irrelevant as a contribution towards explaining how quantity of gold determines quantity of money, and so prices.   For the portion of deposits that represents payments made by customers into their bank accounts plays no real part in expanding or contracting, or otherwise determining the aggregate of purchasing power paid for goods within the year.   On the other hand, the portion of deposits that represents fresh advances to customers does increase the aggregate of purchasing power. If Professor Fisher could show that these advances bore a more or less definite quantitative relation to coins and notes in circulation, or that the power were in any sense based upon the latter, it would of course be an interesting and surprising result.   But whatever is the basis of bank advances, it is evidently not the quantity of coins and notes in circulation. It is therefore difficult to understand how the quantitative relation between ' money,' in Professor Fisher's sense, and deposits has any bearing upon the quantitative relation between gold and aggregate purchasing power.

fresh from mines or banks. The last is the real credit which affects prices.

§ 7. The supply of money, the aggregate of purchasing power expended upon the supply of goods during any given year, consists thus of three contributions.

First and chief, the gross receipts from the payments or purchases made during the year.

Secondly, the additional gold or notes issued as currency during the year.

Thirdly, the additional credit issued as loans, discounts or other advances by banks.

The new capital invested at home or abroad, though it figures financially as stocks and shares with monetary values attached to them, and is for certain purposes regarded as 'credit,' does not as such involve any increase in the volume of purchasing power. The money saved and subscribed as capital to a new Railway Company would, had it not been saved, been spent, *i.e.* applied as purchasing power to 'demand' consumable goods. Being saved and invested, it simply conveys to the Company a power to purchase engines, rails and other capital-goods needed to establish and carry on the business. As such it creates no new volume of purchasing power, but only shifts the direction of its application. Only so far as the stocks and shares may be used by the Company or its shareholders as security for bank credit does this saving and investing process cause or assist the expansion of the aggregate volume of purchasing power.

What the conditions are which underlie the creation of this credit, how far it is based on gold, how far on goods, are questions for discussion later on. At present, it is enough to recognize that such new credit, when it is made, places at the disposal of those who receive it a pur-chasing power not derived from the previous sale of goods.

It may very likely be thought that the dis-tinction here made is unnecessary, because it will be generally admitted that all ' money ' has come either from the mines or from the banks. But such a comment is calculated to dull the edge of our inquiry, which is chiefly concerned, not with the technical origin of monetary forms, but with the sources from which, in a given com-mercial society, the current supply of money comes to those who use it. For this purpose, it is necessary to distinguish clearly the supply which comes in the ordinary course of business, as the gross income, or receipts of money for the sale of goods, from the new supply which comes from the mines or from bank credit.

For when it is maintained that the rise of prices

is due to an acceleration in the supply of money, this will not refer to that portion of the supply of money derived from the previous sale of goods. For an increase in this supply either presumes the rise of prices which it is involved to explain, or, if it arises from a larger number of sales at the same prices, it implies an increase in the quantity of goods equivalent to the increase of money, and so cannot be attended by a rise of prices.

It is, therefore, evident that the increased supply of money which is capable of raising prices must come from one of the two extraneous sources, entering as new gold or new credit. If it can be shown that, since 1896, the increase of new gold coming in as purchasing power, and the new volume of credit (unaccompanied by a corresponding growth of goods), form a large enough addition to the aggregate supply of money to explain a rise of prices amounting to some 20 per cent., the purely monetary explanation will suffice.

The practical questions in this section of the inquiry may be thus stated :—

1. Can it be shown that the recent increased output of gold, by its direct addition to the gross money income of the community, and by its indirect effect in stimulating credit, has caused

an acceleration in the supply of money[1] greater than the acceleration in the supply of goods arising from enlargement and improvement of the arts of industry ?

2. How far are other causes than gold, operating upon the supply of credit, responsible for an acceleration in the supply of money at a more rapid pace than that of the supply of goods ?

[1] It must be kept constantly in mind that supply of goods for the purpose of our discussion means not goods offered for sale, but goods actually sold. Supply of money means not supply in purse or bank, but money actually used for purchases.

CHAPTER III

GOLD AND PRICES

§1. WHEN we are informed that the gold produced during the last fifteen years is a good deal more than a third of the total production since the discovery of America, and four times as great as the production between 1800 and 1850, and that twenty years' production at the present rate will double the gold supply for the world, we seem to have within our reach a sufficient explanation of any rise of prices that has been taking place. The part played by gold as instrument or basis of our monetary system is so imposing that this increased output of gold almost bludgeons the understanding into accepting it as the cause of an acceleration in supply of money great enough to raise prices some 20 per cent.

If the owners of the thousand millions of pounds' worth of gold, got out of the earth in the fifteen years from 1895 to 1910, went into the markets of the world with it, it might appear that their action would have a great effect in raising prices. But let us consider for a moment what the effect would be of this direct increase of the supply of money, to the extent of sixty-seven millions a year.

We have seen that the total quantity of money functioning during a year is comprised of the gross incomes or receipts of all the members of the community plus any new supplies of gold and credit. Now the net income of the British nation alone is roughly computed to be £2,000,000,000. This at a very moderate estimate would imply a gross national income of £10,000,000,000. This sum of money, received within the year as the price of the various goods and services, is the main supply of money expended and operative on prices. To it must rightly be added a large quantity of bank credit. But since no even approximate figure can be given for this, and its origin and mode of creation are not yet discovered, let us leave it out of our account, and look only to the quantity of money consisting of gross income. Suppose, once more (a most generous supposition), that the gross income of this country were one-tenth of the gross income of the whole world, this would give £100,000,000,000 as the quantity of money operative for a year. To this sum there has been added from an extraneous source the gross income

of the gold mines, an amount of £67,000,000.
The gross income from gold-mining will have precisely the same amount of influence on general
prices as the same gross income got from the
textile or metal industries. The effect would
be an increase of the aggregate quantity of money
to the extent of $\frac{67}{100,000}$. The influence upon
prices would thus be considerably less than $\frac{1}{1000}$
or $\frac{1}{10}$ per cent. The actual influence of this addition to money in raising prices would of course
be much less, if allowance were made for the increase of goods which has been going on.

Assuming, then, that the entire output of gold
was directly expended by those who get it from
the mines in purchasing goods, the effect in raising
world-prices would be very trifling.

§ 2. The triviality of the direct effect on prices
thus assigned to gold will be contested by some
economists, who insist that the first effect which
we admit is produced by the additional purchasing
power given by the gold will be continued and
enhanced by subsequent purchases made by
those who receive the first increment of purchasing power.

Mr. Layton, for example, in his able treatise,[1]
discussing the direct effect on prices of an additional million of gold output, traces the first

[1] *An Introduction to the Study of Prices*, p. 34.

effect produced by those who with a million in their purses go into the markets and buy commodities. He continues :—

" But the effect will not stop here : those who have sold the commodities will find that they in their turn have more purchasing power at their command, either because they have sold more goods, or because they have sold the same goods at higher prices; and *they in their turn will therefore make a larger demand on those from whom they purchase.* In this way the gross purchasing power of the community will ultimately be increased by the million pounds multiplied by the number of times it changes hands during the year—the first link in the chain having been the demand of those who had the first claim on the gold."

The error of this reasoning is contained in the statement here italicized.   It is not the case that the first recipients of the £1,000,000 spent by the gold-owners will be in a position to " make a larger demand on those from whom they purchase," so as further to raise prices. This only seems plausible if one assumes that the first expenditure of the £1,000,000 is confined to certain specific orders of commodities, raising the prices of these and leaving others unaffected. If, for instance, we supposed that the miners applied £1,000,000 in increased demand for agricultural produce, we might then assume that the farmers, who received this additional £1,000,000 of income, spent it in their turn upon certain sorts of manufactured goods which had not yet risen in prices, and that, as the result of their increased demand, the price of these manufactured goods rose. The manufacturers in these particular trades, having received £1,000,000 more income, might then be supposed to go with it into the markets and buy, not more agricultural goods (for they have risen in price) but more manufactured goods of other sorts than those which they themselves produce. So, by directing the new stock of purchasing power first to one set of trades, then to another, it might appear to exert the cumulative effect which Mr. Layton claims for it.

But the assumption that it will or can so operate is invalid. This will be seen at once, if we suppose, as we ought, that the first demand made by the mine-owners with their additional £1,000,000 is directed not to any one class of goods, such as agricultural produce, but to all forms of goods in due proportion. The first effect then upon the expenditure of the £1,000,000 will be to raise slightly all prices, say, to the extent of $\frac{1}{100}$ per cent. Now, though the first recipients of the £1,000,000 in the various trades find themselves possessed of a little more purchasing power than before, they will not go into the markets with it and buy more goods. For they will find the prices of all the goods they would seek to buy with their additional purchasing power raised already to a corresponding extent. They will, therefore, not be able to make " a larger demand on those from whom they purchase," in the sense of buying any larger quantity of goods. It is thus evident that the effect of the £1,000,000 in raising prices will be exhausted by its first application, and no cumulative effect occurs. When its initial effect on general prices has been made, the fact that all future transactions must be conducted at the higher price-level will automatically prevent the exertion of any further effect in demanding goods and raising prices. Nor is this limitation really affected by the question, whether the £1,000,000 is expended in the first instance in buying all sorts of commodities or some few specified sorts. Take the extremest of all instances, and suppose the £1,000,000 entirely expended by gold capitalists on diamonds for their wives. This would leave all other prices unaffected, but would raise the price of diamonds to a high level, say, by 20 per cent. The diamond-merchants with their enlarged incomes would buy more of all sorts of other goods ; but the diamond-buying persons in all other industries would find that the rising money incomes they found themselves possessed of, in consequence of the increased buying of the diamond-merchants, were more than offset by the enormous rise in price of diamonds plus the slightly rising prices in all other industries.

In a word, it can make no difference to the direct effect of the £1,000,000 upon general prices, whether it is exerted in the first instance upon a selected group of commodities, or simultaneously upon all groups. It is only the distribution of the effect among the various prices that will differ in the two cases, the aggregate effect on general prices will be the same, and will be entirely compassed by the first exercise of purchasing power on the part of the mine-owners.

Thus it is clear that the increased output of gold within the last fifteen years, though adding very largely to the aggregate amount of gold available for purchasing power, must have exerted a comparatively trivial direct effect in raising prices. Whatever this direct effort may be, it cannot account for more than a small fraction of the actual rise in prices that has taken place.

§ 3. A short cut is sometimes employed to prove

the increased supply of gold to be the cause of
rise of prices. All economic articles, it is said,
exchange with one another in the ratio of their
marginal costs of production. This must apply
to gold as an article which exchanges against
(or purchases) general goods. If the marginal
cost of producing an ounce of gold has been
reduced, while that of producing general goods
has not been correspondingly reduced, an ounce
of gold must purchase a less quantity of general
goods than before, *i.e.* prices must rise. They
must go on rising until the cost of producing
the marginal ounce of gold is again equal to that
of producing a certain smaller quantity of general
goods. For gold-mining is an industry like
any other into which capital and labour enter
for the purpose of earning profits and wages. A
lowering of the cost of producing gold, as compared with the goods produced in other industries, will, by making gold-mining more
remunerative than those others, draw capital
and labour into it in larger quantities. Gold-
mining will receive more, other industries less,
of the new capital and labour available for
industry. This will bring about an increased
output of gold, a reduced output of goods. Thus
prices, the supply of gold being increased more
than the supply of goods, must rise, until the

cost of producing marginal gold is once more equalized to that of producing general goods. The introduction of the cyanide process is usually adduced as the chief instrument for the lowering of the marginal cost of gold production which is the alleged means whereby the rise of prices is effected.

Now let us note the various assumptions upon which this reasoning rests. The cyanide process indisputably tended to allow the profitable working of lower grades of ore than it previously paid to work. It therefore tended to increase, and to some extent must have actually increased, the output of gold. But if each increased output thus automatically brought about a rise of general prices, that rise itself must act as a check upon the further working of lower grade ores, for it will have increased the price of the machinery, stores, fuel, and presumably the wages which constitute the cost of working the gold. Thus, unless we assume a continuous series of technical improvements in mining processes, we cannot account for a continued acceleration of gold output.

" But," it will be replied, " the accelerated output is not in question : it is an admitted fact." That is true. But whether it follows from a reduction of marginal cost of production is not so certain. If gold were an ordinary factory or laboratory product, a cheapening of any process would cheapen the production of all parts of the supply. But this is not the case where an improvement in agriculture or in mining simply lowers the margin of production, letting in a certain amount of new supply from inferior sources. There will be some increase of supply and therefore some effect on prices, but that effect should be smaller in the case of gold than in other articles and sooner exhausted, because of the reaction of the rising prices upon the costs of working the entire industry.

The discovery of new rich mines or layers of ore must probably be held to be a more effective cause of the increased output than the lowering of the margin of production. In truth, so far as the effect in raising prices is concerned, it matters not how the enhanced supply is got, whether by lowering the margin or by an extension of high-grade ores. The increased output of gold will have a proportionate effect on prices. But proportionate to what? Not to the increasing output of gold, but to the supply of purchasing power as an aggregate. In that aggregate £1 of gold has no more direct influence on prices than £1 of any other form of purchasing power. Now gold, as we recognize, plays a small and a diminishing part in the aggregate of money. Its output might go on for a long time increasing at a fairly rapid rate without greatly affecting the aggregate of purchasing power, in which it formed a diminishing proportion. The mere fact that its marginal costs had fallen, or that new rich mines had been discovered, would not necessarily increase appreciably the volume of purchasing power, except upon one supposition. That supposition it is, in fact, that underlies the entire structure of the goldite argument. It is that an increased supply of gold somehow will necessarily expand the volume of credit which is said to be based upon it, and therefore enhances proportionately the entire volume of purchasing power.

It is important to recognize quite distinctly that there is no force in the a priori contention that the cyanide or any other process, by cheapening the cost of producing gold at the former margin, can compel an adjustment of marginal values between gold and goods. Gold is not the chief but a supplementary form of purchasing power, and a lowering of the margin of gold-mining, which only increased somewhat the annual addition to an imperishable article, might continue a long time without making any large

direct addition to the rate of increase of purchasing power as a whole.

Finally, as we have seen, if every economy of
production in gold-mining immediately began to
cause a rise of prices by forcing an increase of
' money,' the effect of this economy in stimulating
output would at once be cancelled by the rising
cost of all the factors of production in gold-mining.

CHAPTER IV

GOLD AND CREDIT

§ 1. THE main contention of those who attribute to the expanding gold supply the rise of prices is based upon an implicit or explicit assumption that every increase of gold produces, or tends to produce, a corresponding increase of credit. Most of the gold, they argue, will naturally flow into the bank reserves, so enlarging the basis upon which is built that great and growing fabric of credit which forms so large a share of modern money.

The bulk of the new supply of gold will distribute itself among the financial centres of the world. Now bankers thrive not by holding large stocks of gold, but by loaning the largest quantity of bank credit they think they can safely loan at the best price they can get for it. An increasing flow of gold from the mines into the bank reserves causes them to seek to induce their customers, the trading, borrowing public, to borrow more bank credit. In order thus to stimulate the increased demand for the money they supply, they

lower the price, *i.e.* the bank rate. Thus a
larger flow of credit passes into the commercial
system. Business men supplement the supply of
money which comes to them in payment for the
goods they sell by this supply of credit. They
use this credit, as all money is used, to buy goods.
It enables them to apply more money in buying
goods than they could otherwise have done, or to
apply it earlier than they could otherwise have
done. It is true they will have to pay it back
again when the time for the credit is exhausted,
but meantime it will have enabled them to earn
more money than they would otherwise have
done, so that the repayment of the loan will still
leave them with some money in their hands to
spend. Moreover, the credit which the banker
loans, though returned to him when the bill or
other advance falls due, will be used with as
little delay as possible for another similar loan,
so that the new supply of bank money, erected
on the basis of the enlarged gold supply, will
continue to swell the aggregate supply of money
available to purchase goods.

The various ways in which a lowering of the
bank rate is held to indicate and to produce an
increase of credit are familiar to business men.

A fall in the bank rate, or price of money in
the Bank of England, is the index of a similar

movement in all the great joint-stock banks whose credits stand in the last resort on the gold reserve in the bank. So the market rate for loans is lowered, and ' money ' is cheapened. Now the primary meaning of this ' money ' in ' the city ' is the advances for a few days made by bankers to bill-brokers. A cheaper and freer supply of money to bill-brokers encourages them to discount bills at low rates, " so that the banks who regulate the money rate thus exercise a strong and direct influence on the discount rate." [1] Not only so, but bankers are large discounters themselves, using brokers as intermediaries and buying from them the bills. They also largely furnish credit for stock exchange purposes to their customers, and especially to stockbrokers who finance the buying and selling of stocks for the investing and gambling public. Finally, the banks make credit advances to business men, merchants, manufacturers, etc., for their temporary convenience in emergencies, or to enable them to take advantage of good business opportunities by enlarging their plant and output, or to seize some favourable turn of the market.

The increased flow of gold which tends to cheapen money induces all these classes of business men who can use bank credit to go to banks and

[1] Withers, *The Meaning of Money*, p. 126.

' buy ' larger quantities of it at the cheaper rate.
This ampler supply of ' money ' they put to
the only use for which money is designed, viz.
to buy goods, services and securities. They
apply in the various markets the enlarged supplies of purchasing powers got from the banks,
and up go prices. At first this rise of prices
will be chiefly in materials, fuel, machinery and
wholesale goods. Later on, the rise will extend
to retail prices and to wages. By the time these
latter prices rise, a large proportion of the increased gold will be drawn from the banks into
ordinary circulation, to support retail and wage
payments at the higher level. Unless the inflow
of gold continues at a rapid rate, the rise of
prices would stop when the increased prices had
become so general that the enlarged volume of
credit, based upon the new gold, had been absorbed in conducting the current volume of transactions upon the higher price level. If, however,
the enlarged influx of gold responsible for the rise
of prices continues, a series of similar effects will
be produced. Prices will continue to rise, if the
volume of money thus manufactured by the
bankers continues to increase faster than the
volume of transactions it is called upon to conduct.

§ 2. This is the usual explanation of the way in

which the increased output of gold has raised and is raising prices. Its simplicity is, however, marred by an unfortunate perverseness in one of the crucial facts of the process. The pivot of the operation is the fall of the bank rate, produced by the pressure of the increasing bullion in the bank reserve. But has the bank rate been lower during the years of this enlarged output of gold, this increased reserve of bullion in the bank, and this rise of prices? Not at all. On the contrary, it has been higher than it was before the influx of gold set in.

The following comparative table makes this manifest :—

	World Production of Gold, fine ozs.	Gold Coin and Bullion in Bank of England (issue department).	Average Rate of Discount.
		£	£
1890	5,749,000	21,818,000	4·523
1891	6,320,000	24,363,000	3·322
1892	7,094,000	25,519,000	2·522
1893	7,619,000	26,425,000	3·058
1894	8,764,000	34,309,000	2·116
1895	9,615,000	38,951,000	2·000
1896	9,784,000	44,334,000	2·478
1897	11,420,000	35,571,000	2·636
1898	13,878,000	33,561,000	3·245
1899	14,838,000	32,268,000	3·753

	World Production of Gold, fine ozs.	Gold Coin and Bullion in Bank of England (issue department).	Average Rate of Discount.
		£	£
1900 . .	12,315,000	33,321,000	3·964
1901 . .	12,626,000	35,830,000	3·722
1902 . .	14,355,000	35,644,000	3·329
1903 . .	15,853,000	34,415,000	3·756
1904 . .	16,808,000	34,412,000	3·297
1905 . .	18,396,000	35,668,000	3·008
1906 . .	19,471,000	33,942,000	4·269
1907 . .	19,977,000	34,917,000	4·927
1908 . .	21,430,000	32,724,000	3·012
1909 . .	21,983,000	32,538,000	3·100
1910 . .	22,023,000	32,081,000	3·725
1911 . .	22,619,000	32,309,000	3·467

A close examination of these columns yields no support whatever to the theory of the causative influence of gold on prices through the bank reserve and the rate of discount, so far as this country is concerned.

Though there was a large increase in the bank reserve in the years immediately following 1894, which appears to follow from the pressure of the increasing gold, the new level attained in 1895 and 1896 was actually higher than in any subsequent year, though the full influx of gold was only just begun.[1] The subsequent enlargements

[1] This abnormal reserve was of course due to the financial crisis of the United States and the disturbance of world finance.

of gold supply in the later 'nineties, and the still more rapid enlargements of the following decade, appear to leave the size of the reserve unaffected. The variations of the rate of discount have no discernible relation to the gold output, or even to the bank reserve. It is true that the beginnings of the new stream of gold into the reserve in 1894 and 1895 are accompanied by a great drop in rate of discount. But the much greater increase of the reserve in 1896 is, for reasons otherwise quite explicable, attended by a considerable rise in discount rate. Generally speaking, it is evident that the average rate of discount, after the new current of gold had definitely set in, is considerably higher than in the years preceding the early 'nineties, and that the group of years with highest rate of discount is the group 1906–11, when the output of gold was at its highest.

In a word, it is quite clear that the enlarging stream of new gold has not flooded our bank reserve, lowering the rate of discount, forcing increased loans of money, and driving up prices in the neat automatic way the gold theorists describe.

On the statistical evidence there is no prima facie case to be made out for any such *modus operandi*.

§ 3. If we carry our statistical inquiry further back, so as to cover the 'seventies and 'eighties in which the yearly output of gold remained virtually stationary, and in which, with the exception of 1876 and 1879, the reserve showed no violent change and no general tendency to increase, the variations of bank rates appear to move with almost complete independence of both sums. A low rate of discount is just as likely to be accompanied by a low reserve as by a high one.

Nor can any connexion be traced during the whole of this period (1870–1911) between rate of discount and prices. As we know, prices fell steadily and persistently from 1874 to 1896. Those who have argued that the cause of this fall of prices was the restriction of the gold supply are confronted by the fact that the rate of discount throughout this period was considerably lower on an average than the rate for the period 1905–11 with its ' phenomenal ' output of gold.

The following quinquennial averages of bank rates are interesting testimony to the apparent disconnexion between output of gold, the course of prices and the rate of discount :—

Years.						Average Discount.
1870–74	.	.	.	.	.	£3·713
1875–79	.	.	.	.	.	3·008
1880–84	.	.	.	.	.	3·384
1885–89	.	.	.	.	.	3·235
1890–94	.	.	.	.	.	3·108
1895–99	.	.	.	.	.	2·822
1900–04	.	.	.	.	.	3·613
1905–09	.	.	.	.	.	3·663
1910–11	.	.	.	.	.	3·596

The only period in which low discount is associated with a large increase of gold output is 1895–99. For the rest, we are confronted by the fact that in the period of small gold output and rapid fall of prices, 1875 to 1894, the average rate of discount is considerably lower than in the last decade 1900–11, when the rapid rise of prices has been accompanied by a great increase of gold.

This brief examination of recent statistical evidence is, of course, not designed as a proof that the output of gold exercises no influence through credit upon prices, but merely to dispose of what may be termed the naïve theory of the relation between gold, credit and prices. That this naïve theory still survives may be shown from the following citation from a recent argument by Professor Ashley : " The most direct and immediate way in which an influx of gold affects trade is by causing the banks to make advances on easier terms, so stimulating enterprise and causing an increase in the demand for commodities and services, and consequently a rise of prices." [1]   Now the increasing flow of gold from the mines during the recent period of rising prices is not seen flooding the bank reserves of this and other European countries, lowering the

[1] *Gold and Prices*, p. 22.

rate of discount and thus stimulating credit, and raising prices.

§4. But the rejection of this naïve theory that gold produces credit does not involve a repudiation of all causative relations between gold and credit. There is abundant evidence connecting expanding bank reserves with expanding credit and with rising prices. It is the order of the causal connexion between these three quantities that is in question. The great output of gold rendered it possible for large flows of gold to pass into bank reserves, if they were wanted there. Whether they were wanted, might depend upon the quantity of credit that was wanted, and which gold would serve to guarantee ; and the quantity of credit wanted might depend upon the profitable uses to which it could be put. These profitable uses might imply high prices, and the increased supply of credit might make these prices higher still. This hypothesis reverses the order of causation usually adopted by the holders of the naïve hypothesis. But it equally explains how a large output of gold, large bank reserves, large credit and high prices may co-exist, as, in fact, we find them. And it has the advantage of explaining how a high rate of discount may intervene between a large bank reserve and a rise of prices. For if we suppose as our starting-point a profitable

use for credit, the large demand for credit this
implies will explain how, even at a higher rate of
discount and of interest, larger borrowings may
take place, these larger borrowings in their turn
calling into the bank reserves whatever portion
of the ampler gold supply is needed to sustain or
guarantee the enlarged credit.   On this hypothesis
gold is not the chief efficient cause or stimulus of the
enlarged credit, but it is, or may be, an essential
or at least a facilitating condition of its production.   If it had not been for the large gold output, it might have been difficult or impossible
to feed the money markets of the world with the
increased quantity of bank-money required to
conduct the volume of trade on its most profitable
basis.

§ 5. The valuable analysis of the distribution of
the new gold among the various financial centres
of the world, and of the notes and loans associated
with it, recently made by the Director of the Mint
at Washington, gives much support to this interpretation of the phenomena.

In the first place, his analysis of the disposal of
the new gold serves to dispel the notion of an
automatic flooding of the bank reserves and a
consequently forced expansion of credit.   It substitutes the guiding principle that gold flows into
those uses and those countries where there is a

demand for it, and that, to understand the effects of the increased output of gold, it is best to investigate the sources of demand.

The Director of the Washington Mint takes two periods for investigation, 1890 to 1899 and 1900 to 1910. His summary of the uses of the new gold in these two periods is as follows :—

FIRST PERIOD, 1890–99

Industrial Arts	$570,000,000
Banks and Treasury of United States . .	260,000,000
European Banks	686,800,000
Banks of Canada, Australasia and South Africa	59,700,000
Total .	1,576,500,000
Other banks, circulation, private holdings, etc.	383,500,000
Total .	1,960,000,000

SECOND PERIOD, 1900–10

Industrial Arts	$958,000,000
India	433,000,000
Egypt	146,000,000
Bank of Japan	69,000,000
Banks and Conversion Funds of South America	343,000,000
Banks of Mexico	28,500,000
Banks and Treasury of the United States .	726,800,000
Banks and Treasury of Canada . . .	85,700,000
Banks of Australasia and South Africa . .	95,600,000
European Banks	863,200,000
	3,748,800,000
Other banks, circulation, private holdings, etc.	288,200,000
Grand Total .	4,037,000,000

During the first period, the decade 1890–99, the production of gold was approximately $900,000,000 greater than in the preceding decade. " The increase was largely taken for the reorganization of monetary systems and for strengthening bank reserves. The gold reserves of European banks increased by 75 per cent., while the paper issues increased less than 5 per cent." Reference to the fuller analysis accompanying this statement shows that loans and discounts of European banks increased about 37 per cent. Of the gold flowing into European bank reserves, amounting to $686,000,000, no less than $535,000,000 was taken by the State banks of Austria-Hungary, Russia and France, the first two being engaged in reorganizing their currencies on a gold basis, the last, France, in accumulating gold in pursuance of the policy it adopted after suspending the free coinage of silver.

The most distinctive feature of the second period is found to be the enormous proportion of the gold which flows into uses that are not directly effective upon world-prices.

Nearly half the aggregate output is placed in this category, including not only the industrial consumption, but the amounts allocated to India, Egypt, Japan, South America and Mexico.

India and Egypt have been rapidly absorbing

larger quantities of gold in the settlement of their trade balances, and that gold does not pass into currency or figure largely in bank reserves, but is hoarded.   The absorbing power of India is noted as a fact of first-class significance.   " In the ten-year period, 1890–99, the net imports plus the country's own production (of gold) were $135,800,000 ; for the eleven years, 1900–10, they aggregated $433,800,000. In the British fiscal year ending March 31, 1911, they amounted to $90,487,000, or about one-quarter of the world's production after the industrial consumption was provided for.   If the ability on the part of India to take and pay for gold proves to be permanent, it is apparent that there will be no over-supply to trouble the rest of the world."

When the Director of the Washington Mint includes Japan and South America in the uses of gold which are " not directly effective upon world-prices," he means apparently that this gold does not pass into circulation or form a basis of note circulation to any appreciable extent.   But in both cases the influx of gold into bank reserves has been accompanied by a large expansion of bank credit in discounts and loans, and thus in-directly may be " effective upon world-prices " so far as it is needed to sustain credit.

The closer analysis shows that for whatever

direct or indirect effects of the enlarged output on world-prices have occurred, we must look outside Europe. For during the eleven-year period, 1900–10, it appears that banks of issue in Europe increased their gold stocks by about 51 per cent. and their note issues about the same, while "their advance on loans and discounts increased about 25 per cent., or by a lower percentage than during the previous period." He does not think that the new gold taken by Europe has greatly enlarged 'the quantity of money,' "going almost wholly to the rehabilitation of monetary systems and to strengthen and buttress the institutions of issue."

"England, sitting at the cross-roads of the world's exchanges, financing enterprises in all quarters of the globe, holding a larger volume of international credits and payments than any other country, presents the anomaly of holding less of the new gold than any other important country. The loans and discounts of her banks increased $450,000,000 with a gain of only $10,000,000 in its reserves."

But while Europe, taken as a whole, has chiefly used the new gold which she has absorbed in reorganizing her monetary systems, and has only exhibited a moderate increase of her 'money' in the shape of coins, notes and loans and discounts,

4

evidently the New World has shown a very great expansion of the various forms of money. The following summary of the Washington table [1] will serve to illustrate this :—

GOLD STOCK

Banks and Treasuries.	December 31, 1889.	December 31, 1899.	December 31, 1910.
	$	$	$
Europe . .	914,396,264	1,601,253,370	2,464,452,800
U.S.A. . .	423,906,282	683,889,570	1,410,721,622
Australasia . .	89,853,167	106,432,311	184,500,000
Canada . .	7,322,710	22,630,659	108,200,000
South Africa .	5,000,000	32,800,000	50,400,000
Japan . . .	...	51,571,000	111,196,000
Grand Total .	1,440,478,423	2,498,576,910	4,329,469,422

NOTES IN CIRCULATION

Banks and Treasuries.	December 31, 1889.	December 31, 1899.	December 31, 1910.
	$	$	$
Europe . .	2,818,198,481	2,973,194,348	4,324,716,358
U.S.A. . .	126,521,364	199,411,492	684,163,511
Australasia . .	29,078,000	21,995,908	107,240,549
Canada . .	32,207,144	41,513,139	82,120,303
South Africa .	5,036,093	9,091,762	8,773,000
Japan . . .	78,871,326	124,779,896	200,009,214
Grand Total .	3,089,914,408	3,369,956,545	5,407,022,935

[1] Supplemented in the case of Japan by an independent estimate of gold stock for 1909 and 1910.

LOANS AND DISCOUNTS

Banks and Treasuries.	December 31, 1889.	December 31, 1899.	December 31, 1910.
	$	$	$
Europe	3,031,196,402	4,184,131,405	5,146,396,802
U.S.A.	3,842,272,131	5,167,895,610	12,855,303,194
Australasia	623,589,889	492,110,885	626,862,333
Canada	149,958,980	251,467,076	870,100,890
South Africa	25,620,935	107,044,970	179,028,958
Japan	109,874,197	501,357,073	915,641,306
Grand Total	7,782,512,534	10,704,007,019	20,593,333,483

Assuming that this analysis of the flow and uses of new gold and of the monetary systems with which it is connected is approximately correct, we are driven to the following conclusions :—

1. That there has been during the period 1889–1910, and especially during the period 1900–10, an extremely large expansion of quantity of money.
2. That this expansion of money has chiefly been an expansion of credit.
3. That this expansion of credit has required and obtained an increased quantity of gold for its support.
4. That the expansion of money has been chiefly operative in North and South

America, and in other new developing parts of the world.

§ 6. The whole drift of this evidence is towards a reversal of the order of causation commonly adopted by the goldites.

Their underlying assumption is that an increased output of gold has power of itself to expand credit and so to force up prices. The evidence as to the disposal of the new gold suggests, upon the contrary, that the initial force is exerted in the shape of a demand for a larger volume of credit, and that this demand draws into the banks of the countries where it is operative the requisite amount of gold to sustain it. Thus the increased quantity of money appears in response to a demand for it.

The phenomenon of primary importance in studying the enlarged quantity of money and the rise of prices with which it is connected, is this rapid new demand for credit in the newly developing countries of the world.

The fact and the nature of this enlarged demand for credit are alike indisputable. If the increased output of gold were closely correspondent in time and in amount with the rise of prices, and if it were the only important economic event that was so correspondent, there would at least be a strong presumption for its causative efficiency.

But coincident with the enlarged output of gold and the rise of prices has been at least one other economic change of first-rate importance, viz. the opening up of large new areas of profitable investment in a number of new countries. It is here perhaps that we find the chief key to the mystery of the rise of prices. Has the enormous new demand for capital to supply the developmental work in these new countries, through its action on the money markets upon the one hand, and the direction of purchasing power on the other, been a chief instrument in the rise of prices ? Let us address ourselves to this hypothesis.

§ 7. Has the area of profitable investment expanded faster than the supply of new capital ? The answer must be in the affirmative, for otherwise it is impossible to explain the rise in the hire price, the interest, of new capital. The actual rise in the rate of interest for recent capital means that the demand for capital has been in excess of the supply at the earlier rate. No other explanation can be given of the fact that 4 per cent. can now be got for whole classes of securities which fifteen years ago yielded only 3 per cent.[1]

How far is this attributable to an acceleration in the expansion of areas of profitable invest-ment or to a retardation in the growth of capital, or to a combination of the two processes ?

In all recent discussions of the fall in prices of Consols and other gilt-edged securities, it has been agreed that a chief cause has been the superior attraction to investors of fairly safe and more remunerative investments in Canada, South America and other foreign countries. Canada and South Africa have within the last fifteen years made enormously rapid calls upon the new savings of this country and the financial world for the development of their natural resources : India, Australasia, Burma and the Straits Settlements have borrowed increasing sums. The Empire has suddenly sprouted with rich financial propositions, which have been brought with growing skill and assiduity to the attention of our investing classes. Not less important has been the appeal of the group of South American countries, with Argentina and Brazil at their head. Japan and now China have joined the band of competitors for new capital.

[1] See "The Rate of Interest since 1844," by Mr. R. A. Macdonald, *Journal of the Statistical Soc.*, Mar. 1912.

Improved communications, fuller and more reliable information, and greater confidence in the fulfilment of financial obligations, have brought new countries into the position of effective borrowers and have improved the borrowing powers of those already in a position to draw upon Western capital. The lesson of repudiation has been learned well, if not perfectly, even by countries subject to violent political upheavals. The technical apparatus of international finance has been greatly improved and extended in its operations. A part of this improvement, indeed, has been the better distribution and utilization of the expanding gold supply. The considerable supplies of gold which have gone to form reserves in Argentina and other countries have certainly assisted to raise their borrowing capacity. But the main factor has been the discovery and opening up of new rich stores of natural resources for the future production of foods and of manufacturing materials. Great new tracts of country have recommended themselves as absorbents of new capital for developmental work and for productive industries. Far more than half of this new work is road-making, chiefly railroads : next comes borrowing by States or Municipalities, largely for roads and other public works :

then mining, and then banks and finance companies. Though oil and rubber have figured largely in the last few years, comparatively little of the total borrowing is for purposes which fully fructify at once or in the near future in useful commodities. The bulk of the application of new capital for overseas investment is for developing lands which will at some later time contribute to the supplies of foods, materials and manufactures of the world.

This wide and deep appeal to the investing public has been synchronous with the new output of gold. But its connexion with it is not very close. For though the capital demanded and supplied is represented in financial figures of stocks and shares, its substance consists in the supplies of engines, machinery, rails and stores, etc., which go to assist labour in foreign lands in the actual work of development.

This recent growth of the market of investments plays, in my judgment, so important a part as a contributory force to the rise of interest, and thus indirectly to the rise of prices, that it may be well to append the following table, showing the extent of the increasing pull of colonial and foreign investments upon our British supply of new capital in recent years.

British Capital Investments (Public Issues)
Percentages [1]

	English.	Indian and Colonial.	Foreign.
1899	53	22	25
1900	80	14	6
1901	75	18	7
1902	56	26	18
1903	39	47	14
1904	40	29	31
1905	31	29	40
1906	30	22	48
1907	25	22	53
1908	26	32	42
1909	14	40	46
1910	19	36	45
1911	16	31	53
1912 (to September) .	24	28	48

§ 8. Starting, then, from the established fact that the period whose price-movement we are investigating has been marked by an immensely rapid expansion of the area of genuinely profitable investments, let us consider what the influence of this fact will have been upon world industry and prices.

It will have two related immediate effects. It will raise the rate of interest, the price of the use of capital rising because the demand has exceeded the supply at the former price. This

[1] *Bankers' Magazine*, vol. lxxxviii. p. 616. Supplemented by figures for 1909–12 furnished by Sir G. Paish.

high rate of invested capital will induce the business classes to borrow more freely from bankers and other manufacturers of 'money,' in order to seize the favourable opportunities of investment which present themselves. If it be admitted that the large output of gold, swelling the bank reserves, stimulates a free supply of cheap money, business men will evidently try to get hold of this cheap money in order to invest it advantageously. This scramble for bank money may go so far and so fast as to counteract the tendency of the 'flow of gold into reserves to depress the rate of discount. A large amount of borrowing may continue at a relatively high rate of discount, provided that the opportunities of new investments are such as to leave a profitable margin on such transactions.

This large borrowing of bank money will go further, if it is wanted not only for financial operations, but also for development of ordinary businesses at home. Now this will be the case. For the capital supplied in such great quantities for developmental work in the new countries materializes in the shape of rails, engines, machinery and stores bought and paid for by the new scrip. The increasing demand in the markets for these materials and goods will have a generally stimulating effect on prices. The coal and iron trades, the machine-making, ship-building and transport trades will feel the first effect of this enlarged demand for concrete capital. All the orthodox indications of improving trade will begin to present themselves. Prices will begin to rise, and there will be an expectancy of further rises. Manufacturers and merchants will now find that trade is profitable, and they too will want to make hay while the sun shines. They will desire to enlarge their productive operations and their output, so as to take advantage of the large sale at high prices. They too will seek to borrow bank money. Their large borrowing will also tend to raise the price of 'money,' which the free flow of gold tended to depress. But the healthy condition of the industrial outlook in an era of rising prices will raise the value of the securities which business men can pledge to the banks, and so the latter can expand the volume of credit which they give to business men.

Another consideration, the full significance of which will be discussed later, conduces towards the same result. This epoch of increasing gold, enlarging investments and rising prices, has also been an epoch in which the combinative forces in modern capitalism have brought about the foundation of trusts, cartels, pools, conferences and trade agreements of various forms and strengths, all designed to raise or hold up prices and increase the margin of profits and dividends in many important trades, and particularly in those engaged in the fundamental industries of mining, machinery and metals, shipbuilding, the transport trades and banking. Here is a separate source of rising prices and remunerative investments.

Thus, both financially and industrially the new areas of profitable investment will stimulate the production of a great increase of purchasing power, manufactured by bankers and financiers, and placed at the disposal of investors and business men. This new volume of credit, representing a rapid large addition to the aggregate supply of money, will be used for the only purpose that money serves, viz. to demand goods. The effect of this large rapid demand for export goods in order to develop Canada and South America, and for machinery, plant and materials in order to enlarge businesses at home, will be further to strain the call upon available supplies and to cause a further rise of prices.

This analysis, starting from the emergence of new areas of profitable enterprise, explains how it is that the increased output of gold flowing into bank reserves has not in fact reduced the price of ' money,' and how in spite of the higher price of money more money has been borrowed. The large influx of gold does not play the directly determinant part claimed for it by goldites. It has not been a chief efficient cause of increase of purchasing power and higher prices. But it has been a favouring condition to this process. For had there been a constriction of the gold supply and bank reserves been low, the price of money would have been higher than it has been, the aggregate amount of borrowing less, the subsequent demand for goods reduced and the rise of prices correspondingly less.

§ 9. But even this limited part assigned to gold as the regulator of the production of purchasing power and so of prices must be subjected to further qualifications.

For synchronous with the recent expansion of profitable capitalism has been an immense extension and improvement in banking and other financial apparatus, alike in the old and the new countries of the world. In the older countries the transformation of an increasing proportion of industrial and commercial undertakings into joint-stock companies with negotiable securities has immensely facilitated the credit system. The development of ordinary banking so as to reach larger areas of the population and lower strata of commerce, the amalgamation of hitherto competing banks, proceeding until in this country a score of companies has absorbed almost the whole business, the expanding part taken by banks in discounting bills and in financing business, the perfection of the clearing-house system, the improved co-operation of banks with one another in crises and the confidence of the great banks that Governments will stand behind them in times of great emergency, signify two important changes in the 'money' situation. First, they imply a great improvement in the negotiable capacity, the mobility, of credit notes of different sorts, a wider and a deeper confidence which induces the ready acceptance of notes and cheques and all orders of negotiable instruments. This is the joint effect of improved financial apparatus and of popular education, and it means increased mobility for all sorts of paper money. Other things equal, this implies that pieces of money will change hands more frequently, or in other words, the same quantity of money-instruments will function as a larger quantity of purchasing power in a given time than it did before.

Secondly, these changes in financial methods diminish the importance of gold, not only in actual currency, but, far more important, for purposes of reserve. Not merely do they allow the building of a larger structure of credit upon

a given quantity of gold, but they impart a degree
of elasticity to the credit system as a whole which,
at any rate in normal times, almost releases it
from any definite gold control. For ordinary banking and finance is being conducted with less and
less regard to that portion of the final reserve in
the Bank of England which consists of gold. This
statement is quite consistent with the maintenance
of a more or less regular relation between the
size of the gold reserve and the rate of discount.
Even in times of abnormal stress the final defensive measures taken by banks, with or without
the co-operation of the Government, indicate a
diminishing belief in the doctrine that gold is the
operative basis of the credit system. It is true
that the movement of gold from London to New
York and from continental centres to London
during the financial crisis of 1907 signifies that
gold still plays a significant part in the monetary
system of the world. But it must be remembered
that it was not only or chiefly the infusion of gold
into the bullion-vaults of America that enabled
recovery and gradually restored confidence. It
was the general confidence that the banks possessed adequate claims upon the real wealth of the
country and would meet these claims. Although
the Clearing-house Certificates, which at such
times the banks have been in the habit of issuing

as mutual guarantees in lieu of specie payment, do not always succeed in satisfying depositors at the time of a panic, they do ease the situation and secure time for creditors to realize that they have adequate assurance of payment if they wait.

§ 10. Before the Royal Commission on Gold and Silver, which in 1887 was investigating the converse of our problem, viz. the persistent fall of prices, Dr. Marshall gave the following summary of his view of the relation between interest, discount and prices : " My position is that the mean rate of discount is governed by the mean rate of interest for long loans ; that again is determined by the extent and the richness of the field for the investment of capital on the one hand, and on the other by the amount of capital seeking investment. The amount of capital has been increasing so fast that, in spite of a great widening of the field of investment, it has forced down the rate of discount. The fall in the rate of discount so caused failed to stimulate speculation, because it was itself caused by the difficulty of finding good openings for speculative investment ; this difficulty being in part due to the fear that prices would go on falling." [1]

Thus was explained the coincidence of a low

[1] Cd. 5512, p. 7.

rate of discount with falling prices. The problem
we have to solve is the converse of this, a high
rate of discount with rising prices. May not the
solution lie along the lines of the same formula ?
May we not say : " The field of investment has
been widening so fast that, in spite of an increasing
amount of capital, it has forced up the rate of
interest and, by a necessary consequence, the rate
of discount " ? This indeed can hardly be called
a hypothetical explanation : it is a statement of
admitted facts. For the price of the use of
loanable capital, like every other price, can only
rise by a scarcity of supply in relation to demand.
Now no one suggests that there has been any
absolute failure in the supply of new capital : on
the contrary, it is admitted that the supply has
been increasing with considerable speed. Therefore the rise of interest can only be due to an
increase in the demand for it proceeding at a still
more rapid rate.

The improved political and economic security
of South American States, the new rich discovery
and development of resources in Canada and South
Africa, the bringing into the area of investment
of vast new tracts of Asia, form new large factors
in this demand for capital. The increased output
of gold indeed affects this enlargement of investments at two points. The South African demand

5

for capital has largely arisen from the goldfields. The improved confidence in South American investments may be attributable in some measure to the large amount of gold which has in recent years flowed into her banks and conversion funds (estimated by the Report of the United States Mint at £68,000,000 during the years 1900–10).

But in the main this enlarged demand for capital must be attributed to the development of concrete opportunities for the production of wealth, an increase of the actual yield per unit of fresh capital as compared with the preceding conditions. The rise of interest is explained, at any rate in large measure, by this appearance of new profitable uses for capital. The large flow of new savings from Great Britain and other old industrial countries into these remunerative fields made fresh capital relatively scarce at home and raised its price. A high rate of interest meant that bank-money could be advantageously employed in buying stocks and shares by those who could get hold of it. Persons with securities to pledge would seek to invest or speculate more freely than in other times. Thus banks and finance companies who manufacture credit would find an increasing demand for this 'money' and this increasing demand would tend to cause them to raise the rate they charged. For though the larger flow of gold into the bank reserves would mean a larger supply of bank-money, that supply would not have grown as fast as the demand.   So it would come to pass that a larger quantity of credit was created for sale at a higher price. Thus the paradox of the failure of the increased output of gold to keep down the rate of discount would be explained.

The next effect would be that the increased quantity of credit would operate in the markets for goods as increased purchasing power.   For the only use of this credit is to buy goods.   The new concrete capital brought into being by the enlarged demand would consist mainly of materials, machinery, food-stuffs and other articles required for the developmental and industrial work in the new borrowing areas, and for ships and other transport work.   But whatever were the actual uses to which the enlarged flow of credit was put, it must primarily operate as new purchasing power in the markets of the world, and its operation would raise the general level of prices.

Now rising prices, however caused, mean profitable trade.   And profitable trade, with high and rising prices, stimulates business men to borrow money, not for speculation but for the enlargement of their business operations.   Thus, as soon as the first effect of the expanding area

of investments in raising prices is felt, that rise
of prices exerts a further stimulative influence
upon demand for 'money' and that increased
output of 'money' carries prices higher. The
psychological nature of this movement is well
recognized. Rising prices, with the expectation
of further rises, stimulates borrowing and buying,
and so helps to fulfil the prophecy.

When, from these or any other causes, the level
of prices has been raised, more credit instruments
will be required to carry on the larger value of
transactions at this higher level. On the theory
that the supply of credit instruments rises and
falls proportionately with the supply of gold to
the reserves, the actual rise of the price of credit
must be interpreted as an admission that the
supply of gold has been inadequate to keep down
the price of money. This interpretation, as we
perceive, is supported by such facts as we possess
with regard to the actual distribution of the
recent gold supply.

This course of reasoning appears to furnish a
more valid explanation of the several sorts of
fact than the gold theory. It does not repudiate
the influence of gold, but it makes it supplementary to the flow of a more vital current of economic
power.

Both have in common the attribution of the

rise of prices to an expansion of purchasing power in the form of credit. But whereas the goldites fail to show how the increasing output of gold expands credit, those who start from the expanding area of sound investments can make good the causal connexion with the money market.

It may then be granted that new gold discoveries and improved methods of treating the ore have greatly enlarged the output, and that this enlargement must continue so long as ounces of new gold can be produced more cheaply and more profitably than the goods which can be bought for their mint price, £3, 18s. 9d. It may also be admitted that the new output makes a small direct addition to the aggregate of purchasing power, and that indirectly through the bank reserves it facilitates the operation of other forces which increase the volume of purchasing power. But there is no ground for attributing to the enlarged output of gold any considerable power to force a rapid rise of prices, or to ascribe the actual rise that is taking place to that cause. The rise of prices, chiefly due to other causes enhancing purchasing power, or retarding the production of goods, acts as a check upon the increasing output of gold which would have been far greater than it has been, but for this diminishing purchasing power of an ounce of gold.

APPENDIX

So much in the foregoing argument depends upon the manner in which plentiful bank credit affects prices, that it may be well here to refer to a view that contravenes that taken here. This view is thus succinctly stated by Mr. Edward R. Pease in a valuable tract, *Gold and State Banking*, issued by the Fabian Society. Speaking of the effect of an increased flow of gold into the Bank Reserve and its effect in lowering discount and interest, he continues: " But low rates of interest mean cheap trading and low prices. So the first effect of more gold is not to raise but to lower, even if only a little, the range of prices." In a footnote, the writer adds: " Some economists argue that a low rate of discount encourages loans for the purchase of commodities and so raise prices. But the new loans may also be applied to the production of more commodities and so lower prices."

Here there is a confusion of thought between the immediate and the subsequent effect of en-larged credit. No such distinction is admissible as is here suggested between loans " for the pur-chase of commodities " and loans " applied to the production of more commodities." Business men who take advantage of relatively low discount to borrow more money, in order to enlarge their productive operations, must apply it in the first instance to increasing the amount of money they use to buy plant, materials and labour, the means of enlarging production. The first effect, therefore, must be to raise the price of the productive goods and services and so to raise the general level of prices. Whether a secondary and subsequent effect may or may not be so large an increase in the output of commodities that general prices fall to a greater extent than they were raised by the first operation of enlarged credit, depends upon the productivity of the new productive goods and services. If the stimulation given to industry by the cheap credit operates largely on trades subject to the so-called law of increasing returns, a fall of prices, greater than the original rise, may ensue. If the new credit operates chiefly on trades subject to the so-called law of diminishing returns, no corresponding fall may ensue. But in any case the first effect of more bank money is to raise prices.

CHAPTER V

THE BASIS OF CREDIT

§ I. WE have now ascertained that, so far as increased quantity of money is responsible for the rise of prices, it consists mainly in expansion of credit. This expansion of credit is not caused by the increased output of gold, though that increased output may be regarded as a necessary condition of expanding credit. To what, then, is it due ? This question has been partly answered by reference to the increased demand for credit for the financial operations involved in the exploitation of new countries.

But that increased demand for capital does not in itself explain how the volume of credit has been created. That explanation is found in an extension of the materials and machinery for the production of credit. Credit is produced by bankers and financiers, out of what ? Not chiefly out of gold, and never merely out of gold. The main staple out of which credit is made is vendible goods, and the extension of credit must be attributed mainly to a growth of the vendible goods which can be used for making it.

That goods, not gold, are the main basis of credit is clear from an examination of the processes of making it.

The following clear account of the leading forms of credit is given by the late Lord Farrer : [1]—

" The debt or credit is either the consideration for goods already sold, or services already rendered, or it is an anticipation of the proceeds of future sales or future services. If I receive bank-notes or gold or a cheque for goods which I sell, or for services which I have rendered, and pay it into my bankers, the credit he gives me, or the debt he owes me, represents the return I get for what I have already sold or done. It is that return turned into a convertible shape, into a promise of the banker's to pay and a right on my part to receive : in legal phraseology, into a right of action against the banker.

" So with respect to credit or debt in respect of future or distant goods and services. What it does, if the credit is sound, is to anticipate the future ; to make the distant present ; and to give what already exists in a potential and in-

[1] *What do we pay with ?* pp. 26, 27.

convertible form the quality of immediate exchangeability and convertibility.

" When a Scottish banker gives a young man credit, what he does is to give him cash and capital for commencing business in return for a promise to pay, which the banker trusts because he has confidence in the future returns to be realized by the young man's capacity, industry and character ; and these are thus, as it were, discounted, and turned into something which their owner can put to present use. The Scottish Bank probably gives this in the form of its own notes, and these remain in circulation until they return to the bank in discharge of the debt.

" When a merchant who is exporting or importing goods, or when a manufacturer who is selling to a dealer, gets a banker to discount his bill, the goods are in existence ; the market also exists ; and the expectation of a sale at a profit may be assumed to be a reasonable expectation. But none of these things are immediately convertible into cash or usable capital until the discount of the bill gives the merchant the power of drawing cheques upon his banker. He therefore has the money or the immediate power of getting it, and the banker has the bill, which he can keep until it is paid, or in case of necessity, can sell or exchange. The cheques on the one hand, and the bill, if it is sold or rediscounted on the other, become additions to the circulating medium until the credit is exhausted and the bill is paid. In neither of these cases, it is true, has the creditor any specific lien. He has only a personal right of action ; but the value of that right and the soundness of the credit depend on the truth of the debtor's anticipations of future realization and profit.''

As regards bank advances, they are usually based upon collateral securities, titles to actual saleable goods. Even when the Scottish banker gives credit on a mere promissory note, the essence of the transaction is the same. The promissory note is in effect a lien upon the receipts from the sale of actual goods which will be marketable at some future time at prices which will yield a profit to the business man to whom the advance is made.

§2. In all the cases where credit is given on goods which either do not yet exist or are not yet marketable, there is of course a risk involved. The credit given does not amount to the full selling value of the goods when they come to be sold. It is less by two separate amounts : first, a deduction in respect of risk, lest the goods should not be sold, or should be sold at a too low price ; secondly, a deduction representing the price for the advance of money, the true discount on the transaction. But the essence of the transaction is that the credit is based upon the actual or anticipated existence of real concrete goods, and that it is measured and limited by the value of those goods.

Where credit is obtained by depositing stocks, shares, or other certificates of value as security, these certificates give a legal claim upon concrete forms of property, the plant, stock and goodwill of some business. Here as elsewhere the substance of the credit is vendible goods.

This is true of every other form of credit or circulating medium, such as exchequer bills, convertible or inconvertible notes, public loans, debenture stocks or shares, etc.[1] So far as any of these is a valid instrument of credit or currency, it has reference to, is based on and measured by some form of concrete wealth, present or prospective, into the possession of which the creditor can enter.

The importance of this essential fact is con-

[1] Where governments create these credit forms they are usually based upon the general body of wealth of the nation over which the government has command by virtue of the taxing power, though sometimes specific forms of public property or income may be hypothecated to their maintenance or repayment.

cealed by the fact that each credit form is expressed in terms of gold and is legally convertible into gold, or notes which in their turn are convertible into gold. So it easily comes to be believed that gold is the substance of the whole credit system, that it is built upon a gold basis, that it can only grow on condition that the gold basis grows, and, finally, that it must grow as the gold basis grows.

Regarded from this standpoint, gold is the stuff out of which bankers manufacture credit : the more gold, the more credit ; the less gold, the less credit.

Now our earlier inquiry into the *modus operandi*, by which gold was supposed to influence prices through the bank rate, led us to suspect the soundness of this theory of the close dependence of volume of credit upon gold. We are now in a position to perceive the true relation of gold to credit.

§ 3. Credit is a form of money manufactured by bankers with the assistance of bill-brokers and other finance agencies. Gold is not the staple material out of which it is manufactured. That staple material is the value of the various sorts of goods (including under that term all marketable goods or claims upon them) as expressed and measured by current or prospective market prices. The fact that these prices are expressed in gold must not deceive us : it is the goods and not the gold that are the basis of the credit. Any article that has a market price is a potential basis of credit, and an increasing proportion of all sorts of goods are becoming available for actual credit. The great increase of general purchasing power taking place in every advanced industrial nation is chiefly due to that fact. Whereas in early banking days only real estate and a few sorts of personality were freely operative for credit purposes, while bills of exchange were very limited in scope, we have now entered an era in which a very large proportion of the whole volume of existing and early prospective wealth carries its regular financial counterpart in the form of credit. A constantly increasing proportion of business is conducted by large firms whose capital is expressed in shares negotiable as a basis for bank credit, or whose separate transactions are of a scale and a publicity accommodated to the credit system.

The perfection of this process would be a business world in which every piece of wealth, land, building, crops, stock, machinery, materials and goods in various stages of production, carried with it a credit-note representing its present value, which could be used when it was wanted. Each specific piece of wealth would have a corresponding token of general wealth attached to it. That token could be used for general purposes of purchase, its recipient holding a claim upon the general wealth into which the specific piece of wealth will be convertible. The volume of credit would evidently expand or contract with the expansion or contraction of the value of the goods which command it, and the notion of an excess or deficiency of 'money' would be meaningless.

But what about gold ? Is the fact, that each of these credit-notes entitles the holder to demand from somebody payment in legal tender, without any significance ? Does gold play no part as an ingredient in the manufacture of these sorts of purchasing power ? Evidently it does. So long as it remains legally possible for the holders of such credit-notes to demand gold for them, while circumstances may conceivably arise which will induce them to use this legal right, some gold must be held to provide against the contingency. As there must be in the ordinary currency sufficient gold to pay for goods, the sellers of which will not take any form of credit-note, so there must be held by banks a reserve of gold to meet the case of those who, having received credit-notes, lose faith in the durability of the purchasing power of these or any other credit forms, and insist upon their legal right to gold.

Gold, then, remains an ingredient in the manufacture of the credit which forms the main volume
of money.   But it is an ingredient of constantly
diminishing importance.   The bulk of the larger
operations of purchase in a modern community
are carried on in all normal times without any
conscious reference to the gold reserves.   If the
confidence of the recipient of a credit-note, that
the goods on which it is based would be sold at a
price which would enable the credit-note to be
redeemed in other credit-notes whose acceptability was undoubted, were absolute, no gold
reserve would be necessary.   So far as this is not
the case, the credit may be considered as manufactured to the extent of, say, 80 per cent. of the
value of the goods, 20 per cent. of the gold held by
a banker.   This proportion which the gold bears
to the goods value is admittedly diminishing.[1]
It may even be questioned whether, so far as the

[1] The recent additions to the Bank Reserves, especially in
the United States, France and England (where the Bank
of England gold reserve has recently been fortified by a
considerable growth of separate reserves kept by the large
joint-stock banks) may seem to contradict this statement.
But this only means that an attempt made to reduce at an
excessive pace the proportion of the gold reserves to the
growing volume of liabilities has produced a reaction in the
shape of a strengthening of those reserves.   This correction
of a temporary excess does not falsify the view that with
the expansion and improvement of the general credit system
a reduction in the percentage of gold to the aggregate of
money is taking place.

internal business of this country and certain others is concerned, the credit system really requires any gold ingredient. So long as the law requires that legal tender ultimately means gold paid over the counter of the Bank of England, gold must no doubt be kept. And this requirement may be a wise policy. But it is by no means evident that it is *economically* necessary as a support for the banking system of the country. If England were a self-sufficing country, no questions of foreign trade entering in, and if the Bank administration were reliable, it is clear that the credit of the Bank itself might prove a quite satisfactory reserve. Inconvertible notes of the Bank would circulate quite freely, being accepted as payment for every debt. That this is so appears from the fact that the knowledge that it is possible for the Government, by suspending the operation of the Bank Charter Act to enable the issuing department of the Bank to issue uncovered notes in excess of the legal limit, or, in extreme cases of panic, the actual suspension, has always in the last resort proved able to restore confidence and to stop a run on gold. This appears to signify that the credit system of this country is based, in its final economic analysis, not on gold but on the real wealth of the country.

Indeed, it is not even true that the existing

6

reserve in the Bank of England which actually supports the general credit of the banking system consists wholly or mainly of gold. Mr. Hartley Withers reminds his readers that " the liabilities of the Banking Department of the Bank of England, which are used as the basis of credit by the rest of the banking community, are represented as to one-half or rather more by securities, and as to the rest by notes, which are again represented as to about one-third by securities." [1]

What the holder of a credit-note wants is a security that the full purchasing power it claims to represent shall be realizable. If a bank, or a government which he knows to be able to secure for its notes this purchasing power, issues them, they are to him ' as good as gold,' even though he is aware that gold could not be got for all of them. His final preference for gold, so far as he has one, is based upon some fear or doubt lest some other persons in the world, from whom he might wish to buy, may entertain some distrust of his credit-note, preferring gold. To that extent the freedom of its purchasing power would be limited. But the credit system stands in the last resort upon the confidence in the ability of the issuer to place the holder of a note in possession of such forms of real wealth as he

[1] *The Meaning of Money*, p. 261.

requires, when he wants it, and in amount such as he expected to be able to obtain when he received the note. Gold is only a requisite to the credit system so far as it is useful to sustain or increase this confidence.

It is a conventional utility, a serviceable check on possible abuses of credit issue, but not in the strict scientific sense an economic necessity in the working of the credit system by which modern commerce is conducted. For international commerce, at any rate with backward countries, it may long be needed. But it ought to be no longer necessary even for international payments between members of advanced commercial nations. There is no reason why the Clearing-House system, which has dispensed with gold in the internal credit operations of the country, should not in the early course of time be extended in the shape of an International Clearing House, all balances on foreign trade between members of civilized nations being paid in Clearing-House certificates.

Such an extension, clearly thinkable, if not easily feasible, makes it evident that gold is not intrinsically essential to the manufacture of credit. The notion that some single valuable commodity must always stand as the background to sustain the credit system has no real

validity. Gold, indeed, is not even now de-
pendent for its position as money upon such
general appreciation of its value as a commodity.
Gold has, indeed, a high but very limited use
for the arts. But this value could by no means
support its pecuniary position. People do not
ultimately ' look to the gold ' behind the credit-
notes because they know that in it they would
have   something   intrinsically   valuable   and
serviceable.   They do not say to themselves,
" I will insist on five gold sovereigns instead of a
Bank of England note, because I know that, if
the worst comes to the worst, I can melt down
my sovereigns and make ornaments or stop teeth
with them."   In fact, of course, any wide
attempt to get industrial use out of sovereigns
withdrawn from currency would soon defeat its
end by driving down to a very low level the
exchange value of gold for uses in the arts.

They call for sovereigns, because they have
more confidence, at the time, in the stable purchasing power of sovereigns than of bank-notes.
" Gold is still the only form of payment that is
certain of acceptance everywhere in times of
crisis." [1] But that confidence, ' credit,' is not
really based on the intrinsic properties of
gold : it is almost as conventional as the smaller

[1] Withers, p. 296.

confidence they still retain in bank-notes.[1] Inconvertible Bank of England notes, if the policy
of withdrawing the gold basis were tolerably
widely understood, would perform all the
necessary purposes of a final reserve for business
operations in this country, passing as freely in
payments of all kinds as gold does now.

If this is not quite ture, it is nearly true, and
its significance consists in pointing clearly to the
truth that gold is not the real or essential basis
of the credit-notes.   It is the marketable quality
of goods and not the stock of gold in bankers'
hands or at bankers' call that enables credit to
come into existence and to operate as purchasing power.   The exact relation in which
gold stands to this credit may still be disput-
able.   " The ordinary language in which it is said
that ' credit ' is an ' economy of gold ' is, even
if accurate, very inadequate.   ' Credit ' is not
merely a means of using less gold.   ' Credit ' or
' debt ' is a substitute for gold as a circulating
medium, which has in some places almost dis-

[1] " The bank finds itself with liabilities which exceed its
cash assets ; but—the excess of liabilities is balanced by
the possession of other assets than cash.   These other assets
of the bank are usually liabilities of business men.   These
liabilities are in turn supported by the assets of business
men.   If we continue to follow up the ultimate basis of the
bank's liabilities we shall find it in the visible, tangible wealth
of the world."—Fisher, *The Purchasing Power of Money*, p. 41.

placed its principal and which may displace it entirely, or almost entirely, as nations advance in commercial aptitude."[1]   Lord Farrer, indeed, in the pamphlet from which we quote, goes so far as to proclaim a doctrine which liberates the production of credit entirely from the control or influence of gold.

" It is a substitute not only of infinitely greater power than the instrument which it replaces, but of infinitely greater expansibility.   There is no limit to its expansion but demand.

" If it is true that exchange by means of credit is barter, the demand must bring with it its own supply.   If goods or services, actual or potential, are to be exchanged with one another, each will necessarily have its representative credit ; and wherever there is a demand for circulating mediums, then there must be an equivalent supply.   There are, no doubt, still provinces which credit has not invaded, and in which gold still reigns with undisputed sway ; and there may be undue contractions as well as expansions of credit.   But if and so far as exchange is carried on by credit, the apprehension of any permanent want or diminution of circulating mediums, or a fall of price consequent on it, is a chimera."[2]

[1] Farrer, *What do we buy with ?* p. 34.
[2] Farrer, p. 35.

But it is by no means necessary to insist upon so full a doctrine of the independence of credit. It may well be conceded that, so long as there remain sections of the commercial world or grades of society where credit-notes are not accepted as readily as gold, a certain quantity of gold may be necessary or convenient as a support for credit, and that for an expanding volume of credit some increase in this gold reserve may be essential or desirable. But while this might imply that an insufficient supply of gold might cripple the development of credit, it would by no means imply that an abundant supply of gold must correspondingly stimulate a development of credit. Granting that a certain amount of gold must stand in the bank reserves as an insurance against collapses of credit, it is not a legitimate inference that an extra flow of gold into the reserves would have power to cause a corresponding increment of credit to come into existence.

§ 4. The results of our inquiry into the increased supply of money may be thus summarized. The direct effect of the increased output of gold upon the volume of money is small. The large increase in the supply of money is due to the expansion of all forms of credit. In the foundation of credit gold is not the main ingredient, nor can an increase of gold stimulate the creation of a proportionate increase of credit. Credit is based on goods and expands with the quantity of goods available as valid security. The increase of credit is due to the facts that (1) the improvement and extension of banking and financial machinery in general, (2) the placing of larger masses of public and private enterprise upon a joint-stock basis, have rendered a largely increased proportion of the general wealth available for credit purposes. The output of gold has been a facilitation in this enlargement of credit, by enabling banks to increase their gold reserves, so avoiding the possible collapses of public confidence in communities where industrial and commercial security were not firmly established.

§ 5. One further point relating to the expansion of credit needs to be made clear. If credit rests on goods, it might appear that every expansion of credit involved a corresponding expansion of goods. If that were the case, how could increased credit be responsible for a rise of prices ? A partial answer has already been given to this question by pointing out that large masses of new credit are due, not to the production of more goods, but to the reorganization of businesses in forms rendering these goods available as securities for credit issues. So long as this change in business structure is proceeding, increased quantities of credit will come into being without any necessarily corresponding increase of goods. That goods in general are expanding along with, and partly as a result of, the new organization of businesses may be taken for granted, but there is no reason to presume that this increase of goods will be commensurate with the increase of credit.

But this is not all. We have spoken of bankers and financiers as the makers of credit. But we have also recognized that the chief financial material out of which they make it is the stocks and shares and other certificates of value which represent the capital created by the saving and investing classes. It is thus the growth of the forms of saving which take these financial shapes that enables the increased credit to emerge from the financial factories. All such modern saving can furnish material for the creation of more credit. No increased volume of goods confronts and corresponds to this credit. This statement is not self-evident, but requires a brief explanation. Income which is ' spent ' passes as purchasing power in exchange for consumable goods. Income which is saved passes as purchasing power in exchange for non-consumable goods, *i.e.* forms of capital fixed or circulating. In both cases alike there is ' real ' income, *i.e.* goods corresponding to the money income, and normally every increase of such money income may be regarded as involving an increase of real income.

But when the saved income, passing by means of share capital, has performed its primary task of purchasing the ' real ' capital, *i.e.* engines, machinery, rails or other capital-goods needed for the industrial or other productive work for which the Company stands, the certificates of this capital remain in the hands of the investors or of those to whom investors have sold them. Now these certificates, accepted by bankers or financiers as security for credit, may cause an extension of credit unaccompanied by any corresponding expansion of goods. This is the principal supply of new material for the financial manufacture of the expanding volume of ' money.'

So long as this process continues, and an increasing proportion of wealth is passing into forms available for credit, the acceleration of supply of money may be expected to exceed that of goods, and prices will continue to rise. If, however, as is possible, a halt in this process, or a reduction of its pace, took place, owing to the fact that most large capitalistic enterprises in advanced countries had effected the desired financial transformation and had secured their credit counterpart, a period of comparative stability of prices might ensue.

But any such slackening of the pace of growth of credit might be offset by an acceleration of the same process in those countries—such as China—newly entering the era of capitalism. If these countries become industrial and take on modern methods of finance, their contribution to the aggregate world-supply of money may be considerably greater than their contribution to the world-supply of goods. In that event prices would continue to rise.

Only when the bulk of the industrial world is so far standardized in its business structure that the greater part of those forms of wealth capable of supporting credit have been brought into the credit system, is there any sure prospect of a reduction in the pace of growth of credit acting on world prices.

§ 6. One final point remains of considerable importance in the relation between credit and the goods upon which credit is based.

The very fact that prices can rise or fall involves the fact that the quantity of credit based upon a given quantity of goods may expand or contract. If, therefore, owing to the expansion of the supply of credit resulting from the extension of banking and the conversion of more businesses into negotiable securities, the volume of money is increased and prices rise, this rise of prices will stimulate a further increase of supply of credit.

For the rise of prices, due to the afore-named causes, will involve a rise in the value of all securities, except those whose fixed rate of interest prevents them from sharing the higher profits which usually accompany rising prices. This rise in value of securities will imply a larger borrowing power, *i.e.* the same quantity of concrete capital-goods will serve as basis for a larger quantity of credit. This increased power of borrowing will be utilized by business men to the full at times when prices are rising and with them profits. This free borrowing will further swell the volume of money and assist a further rise of prices. Thus are brought about the familiar features of a boom in prices, accompanied by a heaping up of credit to a precarious height. For so long as bankers and financiers think they have reason to believe that prices will continue to rise and the margin of profits to expand, they will create and loan more credit per unit of concrete capital offered as securities. Their continued creation of this credit assists to realize the conditions which validate it. But it does not in itself suffice to carry on the process indefinitely. When the real causes which have initiated the rise of prices have worked themselves out, the

artificial inflation, due to a mere anticipation of a
further rise, will receive a check. At the first
sign of such a check in actual rise of prices the
confidence of bankers will shrivel, the process of
issuing more credit on a given quantity of concrete wealth will stop, and will soon lead to a
reverse movement which in its turn will convert
the rise of prices into a fall.

Such is the familiar part played by credit in
booms and depressions. We cite it here, not to
propound any new explanation of the part which
credit plays, but to explain that the fact of credit
being based on goods is quite consistent with a
changing relation between quantity of credit
and the quantity of those kinds of goods which
furnish the credit basis. Part of the recent rise
of prices, so far as it is due to acceleration of
supply of money, may be attributed to an increase
in the quantity of credit which each unit of
negotiable capital supports during a rise of prices.
This is a temporary and adventitious increase of
supply of money and should be distinguished
from that increased credit which is the natural
financial result of enabling larger masses of wealth
to figure as securities.

CHAPTER VI

RETARDATION OF THE SUPPLY OF GOODS

§ 1. A RISE of prices, as we recognize, signifies an increase in the rate of supply of money as compared with the rate of supply of goods, or, if that term be preferred, of transactions. In dealing with an industrial society in which admittedly the absolute rate of supply alike of money and of goods is continually increasing, the causation of a rise of prices is a question of the relative rates of increase in the supply of goods and of money. The facts already cited make it manifest that the supply of gold and of credit instruments has accelerated during the latter part of the period of rising prices. But before deciding to regard this growth of the supply of money as the efficient cause of rise of prices it is necessary to consider whether a retardation in the increase of supply of goods may not have contributed to the result.

That the output of material goods and of services forming the annual supply of wealth has

been continually increasing in modern times, by
reason of the enlarging quantity of labour applied
in more economical methods of production, is
beyond question. Within the last three generations
a larger and larger number of nations have passed
into the modern era of machine-economy; science
has continually brought into use new labour-
saving appliances, and improved communications
have enormously increased the number and
utility of those productive processes which we
term commerce.

The aggregate of goods and of transactions in
the business world has thus been constantly increasing. But the rate of that increase may not
be regular or continually progressive. There may
come times when the pulse of progress beats more
slowly. Or else an increasing proportion of productive energy may, for a time, be put into
branches of production which are relatively
sluggish in their growth and in the value of the
fruit they yield. Or large quantities of productive
power may be allowed to run to waste, or be put
to uses which are unproductive in the sense that
their products do not figure as goods or transactions in the markets of the world, or do not
contribute to the production of more goods or
transactions in the future.

If we are passing through an epoch in which

an increasing proportion of money is expended (1) upon articles whose production conforms to what is termed the law of decreasing returns, (2) upon luxurious goods and services, (3) upon wars and armaments, (4) upon wasteful processes of competition in the distributive processes ; and if, further, (5) high tariffs hamper the productivity of large masses of capital and labour, while (6) combinations of capital and of labour restrain the output in many large organized trades—the aggregate effect of such changes in the application of productive power may be a considerable retardation in the pace of supply of the goods which confront the growing supply of money in the price-equation. We might then discover that the rise of prices was attributable as much to the slower supply of goods as to the faster supply of money.

Although there is no evidence of any halt in the inventive processes which feeds the manufactures or in improvements of business administration in the great staple industries, there is reason to believe that an accumulation of tendencies, whose nature has just been indicated, is operating as a break upon the wealth-production of the world.

§ 2. Though I hold it to be a hopeless task to endeavour to explain a rise or fall of general prices by a series of separate investigations into the causes affecting each several sort of goods, this admission cannot preclude the investigation of phenomena of a wider causality which affect the production and the prices of whole groups or classes of goods. It seems tolerably obvious that, if causes can be adduced explaining a retardation of output in the production of wealth of certain classes or in certain areas, this retardation of supply of goods must *pro tanto* operate in raising the general level of prices.[1]

Let us then take into consideration the tendencies which may be held to contribute to the retardation of the growth of supply of goods.

We have recognized that concurrently with the rise of prices a great expansion of the area of

---

[1] I say this is ' tolerably obvious.' I should speak with more confidence did I not find that the majority of the signers of the Final Report in the Gold and Silver Commission committed themselves to a contrary line of reasoning.

" It does not necessarily follow that the lowering of the cost of production of even a large number of articles would have the effect of lowering the average level of prices, as the saving so effected would create a demand for and so raise the price of other articles."—*Final Report*, p. 23.

The fallaciousness of this statement is easily demonstrated. If the fall of prices of the articles, whose cost of production is reduced, is followed by a proportionate increase of sales, no saving of income is effected, and so no increased demand for other articles follows. If the fall of prices is not so followed, the saving of income of the purchasers is accompanied by a corresponding reduction of income in the classes selling the cheaper articles. There will be no increase in the aggregate demand for ' other articles.'

profitable investments has occurred, and we have seen reason to suppose that this has been an important direct influence in stimulating the supply of credit and so of the volume of purchasing power. It thus tends to raise prices by increasing the volume of money.

But there is also reason to hold that it helps to raise prices by reducing the rate of the supply of goods. This is by no means obvious at first sight. The general effect of the opening up of rich new areas of investment would seem to be an increase in supply. For what else is meant by the development of these new areas except the bringing of new productive agents into the commercial system, and so increasing the world supply of goods ?

This is, no doubt, the ultimate effect. But there are interim effects. In the case of new countries in course of being opened up, a long period of initial development may occur before the harvest of goods begins to be reaped. During this period large masses of capital raised by the investors in the older industrial countries are devoted to making roads and railways, docks and harbours, to clearing land, to irrigation, to building and planting processes, to prospecting and other initial stages of mining, to all those kinds of experimental work necessary to discover

and test the real resources of a country.   Though
the object of all this expenditure is to produce
marketable goods, a long period of capital expenditure, unaccompanied by any considerable
immediate yield of marketable goods, is likely to
occur.

In other words, a large application of the
savings of the industrial world to developmental
work, the product of which will mature later on,
must be attended by a certain sacrifice of present
goods in the shape of immediately consumable
commodities or early maturing forms of capital.
The appearance of these new areas of profitable
investment has stimulated the saving propensities
of the investing classes, so that a larger proportion
of their incomes has been saved instead of being
spent on consumables.   Moreover, of this increased saving a larger proportion has gone into
these late-maturing investments, a smaller proportion into industrial investments producing
goods at an early date.

Of these facts there can be no denial.   The
rising rate of interest has undoubtedly evoked
more saving, and the evidence already cited, as to
the direction of recently invested capital, shows
that a very largely increased proportion of savings
has been going into developmental processes in
South America, Canada, South Africa and Asia.

This increased saving and the new direction of its application must be interpreted primarily as an alteration in the use of industrial power. The pouring of some hundred millions of new capital every year into South America has meant that a corresponding amount of purchasing power, representing the savings of the investing classes, has gone into demanding steel rails, engines, machinery, stores and other capital-goods for export into South America. These goods of course may not be made wholly or mainly by the country providing the new invested capital, but for all that the investment must cause such capital-goods to be created somewhere, for they constitute the real capital which Argentina or Brazil is borrowing.

If, then, it be true that during the last fifteen years an enormously increasing proportion of the new capital of Europe has been invested in Government and Municipal Loans and in Railways and other developmental operations in new countries, the net effect will be an appreciable reduction in the rate of supply of new marketable goods which would have been produced by the expenditure of this money on commodities or capital-goods for home uses. This is of course no indictment of the economy of the proceeding. On the contrary, it is reasonable to expect that

in due course of time the fruits of these investments will come home in quantities of goods which
will lower prices. But in the meantime the
industrial world is pursuing a policy of comparative abstinence, that economy being expressed
in the shape of a retardation of supply of present
marketable goods. I shall doubtless be reminded
that this policy of foreign investment has been
practised a long time, and that the fruits of the
earlier investments have long ripened and are
being garnered in the shape of the increasing
stores of goods and materials that flow into our
markets from the developing areas. This is of
course true. But the issue is one of comparative
pace. The rate of acceleration of recent investments on developmental work has been so
increased that the fruits of the older investments
do not adequately offset the flow of new investments which bear small immediate fruits.

§ 3. Here is one important way in which the new
stream of foreign investment retards the growth
of current marketable goods. But it also acts
in another way, conducive to the same result.
It operates as a constantly increasing demand
for metals, timber, coal and other materials which
form so large a part of the capital-goods required
in developmental industries. It also causes
large numbers of men to be withdrawn from

producing foods and other immediate consumables, and to be applied to the production of these capital-goods. These men, no longer producing goods, must be fed. So this new direction of a larger quantity of income into foreign investments acts as a growing strain upon the agricultural and mining industries.

A larger proportion of the aggregate money income of the world is being expended upon a demand for metals and other materials and foods, a smaller proportion upon manufactured goods. Now this strain upon the industries conformable to the so-called law of diminishing returns involves a decrease in the rate of growth of the aggregate supply of goods, of which they now constitute a relatively more important part. In other words, if the effect of the new investment policy is to cause an increasing proportion of income to be applied to the purchase of raw materials and foods, and a decreasing proportion to manufactured goods, the effect will be to retard the rate of aggregate supply, and so to raise general prices. This movement must be considered to be taking place, though it is masked by the general rise of income and by the *absolute* increase of every order of expenditure. It is the other side of the great expansion of credit in the new countries, and it operates to retard the growth of immediately marketable goods, as the expansion of credit operates to accelerate the growth of money.

§4. If luxuries be considered as comprising all goods and services which by their consumption or use add nothing to the productive resources of the community, it is evident that an increase in the proportion of the aggregate income spent on luxuries retards the growth of goods in general. A community which devoted to the demand for luxuries every increase of its powers of production beyond those required to supply the bare necessaries of life would evidently attain a very slow rate of increase of general wealth, as compared with a community which spent that surplus upon goods which increased the present efficiency of labour, or upon improved instruments of production yielding a quick return in future products. If, therefore, the distribution of wealth in the wealthiest communities and the social tastes and activities associated with the possession of this wealth, combine to cause a greater proportion of the general income to be expended upon luxuries, we are confronted with a real economic force keeping down the actual rate of production.

Now it will hardly be disputed that an increasing proportion of the general income in the advanced nations of the civilized world is going into the purchase of luxuries. Even if, in the face of recent statistics of the respective increase of 'earned' and 'unearned' income in Great Britain and certain other countries, it be contended that the working-classes, taking the industrial world as a whole, are getting a somewhat larger share of the wealth produced than formerly, this admission would by no means dispose of the case. For wasteful expenditure is by no means confined to any one class. Though the proportion of such expenditure will no doubt as a rule vary directly with the size of income, being largest among the richest classes, least among the poor, waste is everywhere widely prevalent. Moreover, as we shall recognize when we consider more closely the effect of the play of recent forces on the distribution of wealth, the general tendency in the period of rising prices has been to increase the share of capital and reduce that of labour, so leaving a reasonable presumption in support of the view that luxurious expenditure is increasing at a faster rate than formerly. If this presumption be correct, it means another force retarding the growth of goods.

§ 5. The growing proportion of the general income of the world expended upon wars and armaments acts as a further and a not inconsiderable check upon the production of marketable goods. The following table [1] shows the growth of the combined expenditure upon Army and Navy by seven leading nations during the period 1881–1911 :—

	1881.	1891.	1901.	1911.
	$	$	$	$
Austria-Hungary .	66,182,000	64,317,000	68,424,000	87,244,000
France . . .	156,154,000	185,448,000	204,580,000	270,908,000
Germany . .	102,509,000	144,434,000	205,785,000	318,446,000
Great Britain .	126,256,000	157,575,000	445,115,000	341,820,000
Italy . . .	49,455,000	80,777,000	78,709,000	120,676,000
Russia . .	103,881,000	142,206,000	208,811,000	319,770,000
United States .	51,654,000	66,589,000	190,728,000	283,086,000
Total .	656,091,000	841,346,000	1,402,152,000	1,741,950,000

The positive destruction of goods which war involves, great though it be, is far less important as a drag upon production of real wealth than the policy of growing expenditure on armaments and the related barriers to free commercial production and intercourse. For the seventy millions taken from the general income of this nation to be spent on the Army and Navy do not simply mean so much wasteful, unproductive expenditure, equivalent to the same sum spent on whisky or on cinematographs. It also means the withdrawal of vast numbers of able-bodied men in the prime of life from the productive services, a waste

[1] Dr. Jordan's *Unseen Empire*, p. 194.

additional to the direct monetary waste of excessive armaments.   It is important to apprehend
this double waste of militarism.   In Europe alone
several millions of actual workers are employed
in producing guns, warships, barracks and other
military and naval equipments, while several
millions more potential workers are employed
in the futile handling of this material apparatus
of destruction.   Though the latter waste may not
have greatly increased during the period of rising
prices which we are investigating, the former has
enormously increased.   The recent growth of
expenditure on armaments has reduced by several
millions of men the effective labour engaged in
the production of goods which figure as supply
in the ordinary markets of the world.   Nor is
that all.   The policy of aggressive or defensive
nationalism with the spirit of mutual fear, sus-
picion and enmity it generates, retards in every
nation it obsesses the application of its full powers
of mind and will to the successful pursuit of
industry.   No people so burdened in spirit and
in purse by militarism can apply itself freely
to the arts of industry so as to utilize to the
best advantage the growing control over the
forces of nature which science places in their
hands.   The concrete barriers set up by such
antagonisms   against   the   free   intercourse   and

co-operation of members of different nationalities impede enormously the productivity of world-industry.

The vast destruction of consumable wealth and of capital during the South African and the Russo-Japanese wars, and the diversion of a large and a growing percentage of the income of almost every great industrial nation into expenditure on armaments, have undoubtedly contributed to keep down the supply of goods which figure in the equation of exchange.

The rapid rate at which in recent years new inventions have been applied in many of the fundamental industries, involving the supply of large quantities of expensive plant and machinery that contain unexhausted funds of utility, is another source of great waste. A very little reflection will show that the pace at which improvements are applied in industry, regarded from the standpoint of industry as a whole, is often very wasteful. Under a competitive system in which the discoverer of some very slight economy can cancel at once the whole value of the existing plant of all his competitors, there can be no provision against such waste. In the case of a public or a private monopoly, improved methods would be introduced at a slower pace which would enable a portion of the unexhausted uses of the older plant to be got out.   That method would be more truly economical.[1]

The rapid application of electricity and other power to traction and to manufactures has no doubt substituted better instruments of production for worse, but such substitution has involved so much scrapping that a temporary retardation of wealth production has occurred.

§ 6. The increasing proportion of the energy of modern nations that is applied to the distributive, as distinguished from the productive trades, must be regarded as tending to keep down the rate of supply of goods.   In all competitive trades an increasing proportion of time, skill, effort and expenditure of every kind is given to marketing the product.   Though industrial

[1] Professor Pigou dismisses this argument as invalid (*Wealth and Welfare*, p. 161).   But his refutation is vitiated by defective analysis of the situation.   A municipality, faced with a proposal to scrap its present expensive plant in favour of a new plant which will work at a slightly lower cost, will properly take into consideration the unexhausted value of the existing plant, upon the capital value of which interest must be paid whether it is scrapped or not.   If that unexhausted value is great, the new plant will rightly be substituted more slowly than if the unexhausted value is small, for the interest on this capital, if considerable, will outweigh a slight economy of working costs in the case of the new plant. In a word, it is evident that the cost of scrapping must enter into the consideration of business policy.   Under competitive industry, however, it is not taken into account.   The former, not the latter, represents the social policy as regards rate of improvements.

statistics afford no absolute proof of such a statement, it is supported by much valid evidence.
The statistics of occupations in Great Britain
and in every other industrial country show the
proportion of the population engaged in wholesale and retail trade, and in other occupations connected with the marketing of goods, to be increasing rapidly. Commercial clerks, shop-assistants,
agents and middlemen of every sort grow in
numbers far faster than the population as a
whole, notwithstanding the concentration of
wholesale and retail business more and more in
large firms.

Such evidence may not, indeed, be in itself
convincing proof of an excessive quantity of
distributors. For it might be contended that,
since the great technical economies of modern
factories and workshops are not to any great
extent applicable to the distributive processes,
it was only to be expected that the latter should
absorb an increasing proportion of the working
population. The mere increase of persons employed in wholesale and retail trade is no positive
proof of waste.

Probably the concensus of opinion among
business men to the effect that more and more
of their effort, skill and expenditure goes to the
marketing of their goods is more convincing

evidence. It is generally held that of the retail price paid by consumers for most sorts of goods an increasing proportion goes as costs of marketing, not merely in the retail but in the earlier stages.

Some striking evidence upon this head was issued in a recent report of the Department of Agriculture in the United States, from which it appeared that in the case of beef the intermediate and the final selling costs added 91⅔ per cent. to the true cost of production, and that just half the retail price of milk went to the dealer and the dairyman. Fruit and vegetables, it is believed, often yield a similarly small proportion of the retail price to the producers.

Such cases, however, of the manipulation of foods or other perishable goods, may be explicable in other ways not involving the assumption that an increasing amount of work or of workers is engaged in their distribution. So far, indeed, as retail trade is concerned, such evidence of comparisons between wholesale and retail prices as is procurable in this country does not indicate any large increase in the proportion of the final price absorbed in retail trade. Retail trade seems to live upon a narrow profit on a large turnover. Probably the increased expense of marketing is found more in advertising and in agents' allowances than in retail shopkeeping.

But the general body of testimony to the increasing waste of competitive energy in the distributive processes is too strong to be gainsaid. The increasing difficulty which a small business man finds of setting up in any productive industry with the least prospect of success, and the comparative ease with which he can obtain goods and credit for distributive work as an agent or shopkeeper, are certainly driving excessive numbers of men into the latter processes. How much importance may be attached to this phenomenon, and how far it has been growing during the last fifteen years, may be open to question. But the withdrawal of large and increasing proportions of the population from productive into distributive work must have some appreciable effect in retarding the growth of goods, the issue with which we are here concerned.

§ 7. To the higher tariffs which have prevailed of late years in the protective countries of Europe and America must be ascribed some considerable influence in retarding the productivity of those countries, and indirectly in reducing the rate of productive progress for the industrial world, by impairing the efficient division of labour, which is the result of free trade.

This raising of tariffs has been fairly coincident with the modern rise of prices. The Dingley

Act of 1897 imposed a higher general rate of duties than had ever prevailed before, applicable to a large and increasing population whose dependence upon foreign sources for many of their supplies was growing rapidly. That general level of high duties was not reduced by the Aldrich Tariff of 1909. Though the Canadian high tariff system began earlier and was not increased during the last two decades, the increasing dependence of Canada upon foreign trade has enhanced the amount of damage her protective system has inflicted. The recent German policy, dating from 1902, has been one of largely increased stringency, while the considerable advance in protective duties in France since 1892 has been a marked feature of her economic policy.

The tariff policy, in its bearing upon the prices of the protected country, is notorious and within limits measurable. The rise of import duties in so many of the most populous and productive countries has, of course, a direct effect in raising prices in those countries. To some not inconsiderable extent it may serve to lower certain prices in free-trade countries. The obstruction offered, for example, to the entrance of food imports into France and Germany enlarges the supply that finds its way into this country, and keeps the prices down in our markets. In considering the net effect of protection upon world-prices and world-production, this partial offset must be kept in mind. But, nevertheless, there is a large and a growing amount of injury done to the volume of world-production by the higher tariff policy adopted by so many countries whose free co-operation and intercourse are necessary to maintain the highest pace of industrial progress. The increased protection of the last two decades may be taken as a considerable cause of the retardation of supply of goods to the markets of the world.

§8. The growth of trusts, cartels and various orders and degrees of combination in many great organized trades in Europe and North America can only be interpreted as restraints upon supply of goods. Their *raison d'être* is the maintenance of prices on a profitable basis by limitation of supply. For in no other way can profitable prices be maintained. The tendency towards so-called over-production has been the invariable plea for the utility of these organizations. They must, therefore, be understood as instruments for keeping the rate of supply of goods in the industries where they operate lower than it would have been had they not existed. Though there are other economies of combination, this is the main and essential result —to regulate, *i.e.* to retard, production.

8

In the United States and Germany, especially, no small portion of the rise of prices of foods, fuel and various sorts of manufactured goods is attributed specifically to the action of 'combines.' This rise of prices can only be compassed by making goods relatively scarce, *i.e.* by reducing the rate of their supply.

Now the 'combine' movement, especially in North America, Germany and Austria, has made exceedingly rapid advances in the last fifteen years. Organically connected with the tariff policy, it may certainly be regarded as a *vera causa* of rising prices during the period we have under special survey.

We find, then, a number of causes, some acting separately, some in conjunction, co-operating to retard the production of goods during the period of rising prices. May not this retardation thus brought about be considered as important a cause of the rise of prices as the acceleration of the supply of money ?

CHAPTER VII

THE DISTRIBUTION OF WEALTH

§ 1. THE rise of prices has been accompanied by changes in the distribution of wealth which are causing grave discontent among the working classes of the advanced industrial nations. If rising prices affected equally and immediately all sorts of goods and services, they would be a matter of indifference, except that they might present a delusive appearance of general prosperity to persons habituated to reckon prosperity in terms of money rather than of money's worth. But rising prices affect different classes of income and property very differently. The broadest and most obvious distinction is that between fixed and variable incomes. Money incomes, fixed by law, agreement or custom, shrink in their value with a rise of prices. Persons living upon the interest of Consols or other public funds, preference shares or debentures or public companies, mortgages, pensions, loans, leases or other fixed payments, suffer losses proportionate

to the rise of prices. Others, living upon payments
slowly adjustable, suffer loss according as the rise
of price is more rapid than the process of adjustment. Such is the case with most professional
men and officials, living upon fees or salaries,
and with large bodies of employees in railways and
other transport services, the profits of which are
derived from tolls or rates which are relatively
fixed. Persons whose incomes are obtained by
selling goods and services, for sums not fixed by
law, contract or custom, but varying quickly with
the conditions of the market, ought, in strict
economic theory, to suffer no injury from a rise
of prices. Indeed they ought to be gainers to
some extent, reaping a benefit at the expense of
the persons with fixed incomes. In some cases
this evidently happens. In businesses where the
capital consists partly of debentures and preference
shares, partly of ordinary shares, the holders of
the latter have certainly gained by the reduction
in the ' real ' interest paid on the former. Every
debtor, in fact, has gained, and every creditor has
lost, where the terms of the loan were fixed before
the rise of prices occurred, or where, being fixed
during the rise of prices, they failed to take into
account the probability of further rises.

Since most creditors are relatively rich and most
debtors relatively poor, it might appear that this

result of rising prices would tend towards a more even apportionment of wealth. And so no doubt it would if the rise of prices had been equally applicable to all sorts of goods and services. But it has not. The prices of some classes of commodities have risen much more than those of others. As regards the consumable or final commodities upon which the greater part of most incomes is expended, the most necessary classes of commodities have been subjected to the highest rises of price. The prices of the foods, fuel and shelter, upon which the workers spend the largest proportion of their incomes, have risen more than the prices of most articles of comfort or luxury which figure largely in the expenditure of the wealthier classes.

A comparison of the effective purchasing power of four incomes of, respectively, £10,000, £1000, £150 and £50 per annum, would show that the loss of purchasing power due to the rise of prices varied inversely with the size of the income. In the £10,000 income the margin for saving and investment would be large, and large bodies of the stocks and shares bought by such savings have fallen in price. Of the expenditure a large proportion will be applied to luxurious goods and services, which have either not increased at all in price or not commensurately with ordinary food-

stuffs. While in the £1000 income the proportion of expenditure upon articles of which
the price has risen would be larger and the margin
of saving and investment smaller, the net damage
inflicted would still be small, especially when
expressed in the total utility of the income. On
such an income the rise of prices would not
involve any curtailment of a necessary or a prime
convenience of life, but would only reduce the
expenditure upon unnecessaries. In the case of
the lower incomes, the expenditure on articles
such as food, fuel and rent, the price of which
has greatly risen, absorbs the greater part of the
income. In the case of the £50 income quite
four-fifths would ordinarily be expended in these
ways. Thus it appears that the rise of prices
presses with double effect upon the poorer grades
of society, first, because it affects a larger proportion of their income; secondly, because a reduction of their real income of a given amount,
say 20 per cent., involves a greater reduction
in the net utility of that income than the
same reduction in the case of a higher real
income.

§ 2. Even if money wages had risen equally with
the general level of prices, this excessive rise of
food prices would have involved some loss to the
wage-earners. But the most significant feature

in the recent situation has been the failure of
money wages to keep pace with the rise of food
prices in the countries from which reliable returns
are available. The following table gives the
official measurements of wages and food prices
in Great Britain founded upon the base year
1900.

The index numbers are founded on the prices
and the amount of wages current in the base
year 1900.

Year.	Food and Drink.	Wages.	Year.	Food and Drink.	Wages.
1879 .	141·4	83·3	1896 .	93·3	89·9
1880 .	141·8	83·2	1897 .	97·4	90·8
1881 .	139·5	84·7	1898 .	102·3	93·2
1882 .	142·1	85·8	1899 .	98·1	95·3
1883 .	141·2	85·8	1900 .	**100·0**	**100·0**
1884 .	124·9	85·0	1901 .	100·4	99·0
1885 .	116·5	83·6	1902 .	101·7	97·7
1886 .	110·9	82·8	1903 .	100·7	97·2
1887 .	107·8	83·0	1904 .	101·4	96·6
1888 .	111·9	84·7	1905 .	101·2	97·0
1889 .	111·3	87·5	1906 .	100·5	98·4
1890 .	109·5	90·2	1907 .	105·1	101·7
1891 .	117·0	91·5	1908 .	106·6	101·2
1892 .	110·9	90·0	1909 .	108·7	99·9
1893 .	109·7	90·1	1910 .	109·0	100·2
1894 .	102·9	89·4	1911 .	111·6	100·3
1895 .	99·5	89·1			

Dividing the years covered by this table into

two periods, that of steady or falling prices from 1879 to 1896, and that of rising prices from 1897 to 1911, we recognize that the rise of prices has meant a decided loss in real wages. 1912, however, has been a year of rising money wages in many trades, and it is probable that, when reliable averages are available for price and wage changes during the year, a not inconsiderable rise of real wages will be seen to have occurred. For though throughout both periods money wages have been rising, and rising faster in the period of rising prices, their rise has not equalled the rise of prices. From the opening of the second period the rise in real wages, persistent during several generations, was brought to a standstill, and during the first decade of the country a net loss of real wages has been sustained.

The rise of prices, however caused, has been accompanied first by a stoppage in the progress of the workers, and afterwards by a positive retrogression in the real remuneration of their labour.

An interesting table prepared by Mr. G. H. Wood,[1] and arriving at a closer calculation of variations of actual earnings by reference to retail prices of commodities, with an allowance for

[1] *Statistical Journal,* March 1909.

unemployment in the estimate of money wages, corroborates this general conclusion.

Year.	Average Money Wages.	Average Retail Prices.	Real Wages, allowing for Unemployment.
1879 . .	146	103	121
1880 . .	147	107	127
1881 . .	147	105	131
1882 . .	147	106	132
1883 . .	149	102	136
1884 . .	150	100	132
1885 . .	149	96	134
1886 . .	148	92	136
1887 . .	149	89	143
1888 . .	151	89	149
1889 . .	156	91	155
1890 . .	163	91	162
1891 . .	163	92	159
1892 . .	162	92	153
1893 . .	162	89	155
1894 . .	162	87	158
1895 . .	162	84	163
1896 . .	163	83	170
1897 . .	166	86	170
1898 . .	167	87	169
1899 . .	172	86	176
1900 . .	179	89	179
1901 . .	179	90	175
1902 . .	176	91	170
1903 . .	174	92	164
1904 . .	173	93	160
1905 . .	174	92	163
1906 . .	176	92	168
1907 . .	182	95	170
1908 . .	181	97	159
1909 . .	179	97	157
1910 . .	$179\frac{1}{2}$	98	161

It shows real wages advancing with fair regularity and increasing rapidity from 1879 to a period of climax lasting from 1896 to 1900, and then undergoing a considerable fall. This table is so interesting that it may be well to present the portion of it which must closely concern our current problem.

The base year is 1850, but we omit the earlier statistics and begin with the year 1879, which is taken in the earlier official table.

§ 3. But whatever standard for estimating real wages is taken, it is seen that the rise of prices has been the signal for a stoppage of the rise of real wages which had been taking place, with a few slight breaks, during the previous generation. During the opening decade of this century a positive decline of real wages has taken place in Great Britain. In various degrees the same is true of the real wages of the working classes in the United States and Canada, in France, Germany and Italy. In some cases the loss of real wages has been considerable, in others trifling, but this century has seen a weakening of the economic standard of life throughout the developed sections of the industrial world.

Now this might be attributed to the pressure of a growing population in these countries upon the supply of wealth. If the growth of world-wealth barely kept pace with the growth of population it might seem natural and necessary that wages should not rise, and if population outstepped production it might seem that wages must fall. Our analysis of certain forces acting to retard the rate of growth of wealth might seem to countenance some such interpretation.

But though we have seen reason to believe that some slackening in the increased pace of wealth production has been taking place, it is impossible to acquiesce in this interpretation in face of certain plainly admitted facts relating to the growth of incomes and of property. While money wages have been stationary in Great Britain during this century, the aggregate income of the nation has grown at a far faster pace than the population, as attested by every evidence of foreign trade, income assessed for income tax, railway and banking returns. There has been a considerable enlargement of the national dividend, but labour has been getting a relatively smaller share. If anyone is disposed to cavil at the adequacy of this cumulative evidence that capital is getting a relatively larger, labour a relatively smaller, share, there remains the clinching testimony of the rise of interest.

The rate of interest upon current investments in Consols and first-class debentures in this country steadily fell for more than thirty years preceding 1896, and since that time they have risen to an extent of at least 25 per cent.[1]   The rise in the rate of interest on capital thus synchronizes closely with the fall of real wages.   This can be no accident.   Its meaning is unmistakable. Treating capital and labour as participants of the national dividend, it can only mean that a shift in the distribution has taken place, labour taking less and capital more.

The hire price of capital has risen at least equivalently to the rise of general prices : the hire price of labour has either fallen or has not risen at all.

It is this stagnation or fall of real wages that is stirring the discontent of the workers everywhere. In this and other advanced industrial countries most classes of wage-earners had made considerable and fairly continuous rises of real wages during half a century, and the expectation of further advances underlay their common attitude towards the future.   Suddenly this expectation is baffled, and instead of advance they experience retrogression in the standard of living.   Trade unionism, with its policy of collective bargains, the newly-won representation of labour by working-men in Parliament, the advance of

[1] See R. A. Macdonald, "The Rate of Interest since 1844," *Statistical Journal*, March 1912.

PRICES OF BONDS, STOCKS AND COMMODITIES (U.S.A.)

(Reproduced by permission of the Editor from "Cotton and Finance")

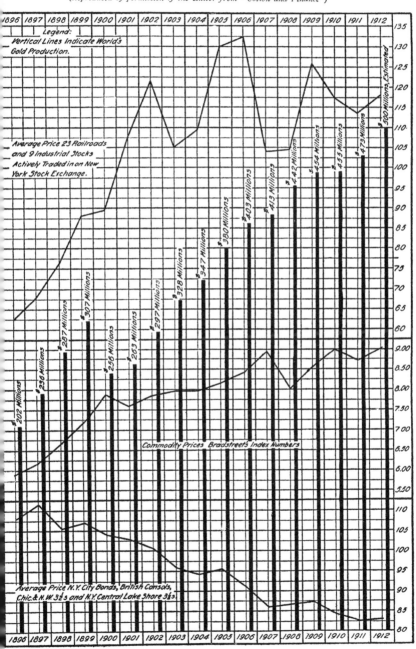

Legend:
Vertical Lines Indicate World's
Gold Production.

Average Price 23 Railroads
and 9 Industrial Stocks
Actively Traded in on New
York Stock Exchange.

Commodity Prices Bradstreet's Index Numbers

Average Price N.Y. City Bonds, British Consols,
Chic. & N.W. 3½'s and N.Y. Central Lake Shore 3½'s

$202 Millions
$236 Millions
$287 Millions
$307 Millions
$256 Millions
$263 Millions
$297 Millions
$328 Millions
$347 Millions
$350 Millions
$403 Millions
$413 Millions
$442 Millions
$454 Millions
$455 Millions
$473 Millions
$500 Millions, Estimated

State and Municipal Socialism seem to avail nothing against this insidious attack upon their standard wages by the rise of prices.

§ 4. It has been generally admitted that a rise of prices is detrimental to labour in that there is a ' lag ' in the rise of wages. If prices continue to rise faster than wages, that ' lag ' may involve a considerable loss to labour. It may even break down the standard of comfort and of productive efficiency of whole classes of workers, and so, impairing future productivity, make for a further rise of prices with further injuries to the real incomes of the workers. It is, therefore, of importance to ascertain, if we can, why wages, the price of labour, have failed to rise correspondingly with other prices. So far as the ' lag ' theory is an explanation, not a mere statement of a fact, it implies a slowness of the workers to demand a rise of money wages which the circumstances of their trade would enable them to secure, if they demanded it. Now, granting this inertia of labour to exist, it is certainly much lessened by trade unionism and the habit of collective bargaining. Labour has been more frequently charged with making and pressing excessive demands for higher wages than with remaining acquiescent in a customary wage during long periods of rising prices.

It seems reasonable, then, to look for other explanations of the smaller share of the product which labour appears to be receiving. If land, capital and business ability are getting higher prices and a larger total share, must this not be due to the fact that the owners of these factors of production are in a stronger bargaining position relative to labour than formerly ? If production in recent years is making greatly increasing demands upon the natural resources of the soil, for foods and raw materials to sustain the great increases of population which modern immigration has been placing upon the lands of North and South America and for the developmental work which is going on, and if city life has been absorbing enormous masses of the population either in old or new countries, there is reason to believe that rent of land must be gaining an increasing proportion of the dividend of world-wealth. But so far as the older settled countries are concerned, though the increasing proportion of town-dwellers has brought a large rise of land values, the great increase of incomes of the well-to-do classes has been drawn from capital and the control of capitalist industry. Though some part of this increase may be attributed to the larger number of industries which have passed into the area of capitalistic enterprise, and the constantly increasing quantity of capital employed to co-operate with each unit of labour-power, the rising rate of interest indicates that this is not an adequate measure of the new power of capital. The rise in the price of new capital during recent years can only be explained, in terms of the general law of price, as due to a relative scarcity of supply. Notwithstanding the great savings effected by the richer classes in the advanced industrial nations, the supply of new capital has evidently been unequal to the demand at the older rate of interest. In other words, there has been a relative scarcity of capital. Part of the rise in interest and profits is probably thus explained. But not the whole. In some countries it is manifest that the high earnings of large masses of industrial and commercial capital are due, not so much to what may be termed a natural scarcity, as to the limitation of competition between the owners of capital, *i.e.* the organization of industry for limiting output, maintaining profitable prices and bargaining with labour.

Part of the rising interest and profits are due to the establishment over large markets of prices above the level which free competition would have maintained. The era of large gold output, of expanding credit and of new large productive

areas of investment, has also been the era of
trusts, cartels, conferences and combines of
every size and strength, all directed primarily to
secure a higher rate of interest and profit than
competition would secure for the group of businesses engaging in the operation. Tariffs, railroads, ownership of rich natural resources,
control of the credit system, public franchises and
contracts, political influence for opportunities of
foreign investment and preferences in foreign
markets, these and other economic and political
instruments have been utilized by capitalists and
business men in order to place large masses of
capital in employments containing some measure
of monopoly, and the interest and profit gained
from such employment form an increasing proportion of the unearned incomes of the well-to-do
classes of Europe and America.

The era of competition in the business world is
giving place more and more to an era of combination. While capital and labour are both
combining, the combination of capital is advancing faster and is more effective. Though
primarily designed more for the control of output
and of selling prices than for bargaining with
labour, it has been inevitable that trusts, and
other combines or federations of businesses,
should pay increasing attention to the art of

buying labour economically. Though this art, intelligently practised, involves the payment of a wage of subsistence and other minimum conditions for labour, it also involves a rigorous interpretation of subsistence and a determination to prevent rises of wages from encroaching upon profits. This new organization of capital thus tends to militate against the rise of wages in two ways : by restraining competition in the markets so as to raise the price of the commodities which wages buy, and by restraining money wages from rising so as to compensate the workers adequately for the rise of prices. Though there is here no closely thought-out and conscious policy, the operation of organized modern capitalism is towards a modified ' iron law of wages,' keeping real remuneration of labour down to a level of minimum efficiency demanded for the sorts of skilled or unskilled labour which the several industries require.

The relative scarcity of capital in the advanced industrial countries is a natural result of the greater mobility of capital as compared with labour. It would seem to imply as its necessary counterpart a relative abundance of capital in the new developing countries which receive the flow of foreign capital, and probably a higher rate of wages in these countries than would otherwise

9

have prevailed. Though in the United States and Canada the growth of trusts and other combines, together with the operation of high protection, appears to have reduced real wages during recent years, it is certain that the abundant flow of overseas capital has tended to counteract these influences. Moreover, it must be remembered that the large increase of wage-earning population in these countries means that a larger proportion of workers in the industrial world are working in countries where a high level of real wages prevails. If reliable statistics for South America were available, we should almost certainly discover that a rise of real wages for a rapidly increasing number of workers had been taking place.

§ 5. As a larger quantity of the important industries in a larger number of countries pass into a condition where machinery and other capitalistic methods are of growing importance, it follows that, though no change occurs in the rate of remuneration per unit of capital and labour, an increasing proportion of the total product would go to capital. Capital ' does ' relatively more, labour less. If, in addition, capital is relatively scarce, or is better organized, the payment per unit for this larger capital will be greater, and that for labour smaller. This appears to have been happening in recent years in the advanced countries, as the rise of real interest and the fall of real wages testify.

So far as the issue on its world-scale is left to the free play of economic forces, its future depends upon the factors determining the relative supply and demand for capital and labour. Though, at the present juncture, capital appears to have the upper hand, the causes of this superiority may not be long-lasting. If our analysis of the situation is correct, the primary causes are (1) a rapid new demand for large amounts of capital to assist in developmental work at a time when great wastes of capital and of current expenditure have been taking place, and (2) a rapid improvement in the industrial, commercial and financial organization of capital, enabling large masses of it so to temper competition by combination as to obtain a profitable control of markets and stronger powers of bargaining with labour. The rise of prices has been of considerable secondary service in strengthening the pull of capital, and incidentally of land and business enterprise, upon the product.

How long this superiority of capital will last depends chiefly upon (1) the nature and pace of industrial improvements requiring increasing quantities of capital per unit of labour, *i.e.* the future of labour-saving machines and methods;

(2) the quantity of developmental work still remaining to be done; (3) the quantity of labour available for co-operation with capital in the various countries where it is required.

To these highly speculative questions no clear answer can be given.   There are, however, certain changes in the strength of these determinant factors which are likely.   If we are right in our analysis of the nature of the overseas investments, it is to be expected that, when they fully fructify in increases of consumable goods, there will be a fall of prices especially affecting food supplies. Such a fall of prices would in itself act as a check upon the rate of further developmental work, leaving a larger proportion of new savings for investment in home enterprises, and lowering again the rate of interest.   If, as is probable, the best available areas for profitable development have already been tapped and opened up by the enterprise of the last two decades, the future over-seas investment will be on a scale of diminishing returns, exercising a further check upon this slowly-fructifying order of investment.   Though the world may contain unexplored resources as large and valuable as any yet discovered, it is at least likely that a considerable pause will ensue upon the abnormally rapid movement of the last years.

§ 6. Whether any such reduction in the pace of world-development is likely to be compensated by an increasing demand for capital due to further increments of labour-saving inventions is a quite open question. On the one hand, it might seem that, after a certain progress had been made in raising the great primary manufactures through the world to a standard of high mechanical efficiency, further increments must be on a descending scale, and that this same economy would apply to transport. On the other hand, it is arguable that as there is no assignable limit to the useful application of the sciences to industry, and as modern education and intercourse place the inventive intelligence of mankind upon a better basis of co-operation, we may expect a quickening of the pace of discovery and the rate of technical improvements. If this be so, may not capital continue to be relatively scarce and to demand and obtain a high rate of interest measuring its scarcity ?

Against this we may perhaps set two not unimportant considerations. As a larger proportion of the world becomes developed and standardized for modern economic work and life, the actual amount of wealth in the hands of the classes capable of saving will grow rapidly. Even allowing for the rising standard of luxury, the amount, and probably the proportion, of the savings of these classes will grow. The new developing countries which have been taking so much of the new capital from the older countries will soon be in a position to supply themselves from their own resources. Unless, therefore, we assume the above-named causes increasing the demand for capital to be continuously operative, the increasing supplies of capital may be so great as once more to restore the condition of falling rate of interest which prevailed during most of the nineteenth century.

The other counteracting tendency to the economic domination of capital is the reduction of the supply of labour due to a reduced growth of working-class populations. In all advanced nations a distinct and progressive fall of the birth-rate and a reduction in the net growth of population are discernible. As an increasing proportion of the total volume of labour power comes under this influence, a scarcity of supply of labour may make an appreciable effect upon its market price over a larger area of the industrial world. Though the increased intensity and efficiency of labour may in some measure counteract this tendency, that again may be offset by a reduction in the hours of labour.

§ 7. Finally, two factors of immeasurable im-

portance must be kept in mind in any attempt
to speculate upon the future distribution of
world-wealth. One is the growing part likely
to be played in the near future by the employment of capital and labour in public enterprises.
The State and the Municipality are evidently
destined to employ an increasing proportion of
the total supply of the factors of production, and
so far as the distribution of this product is concerned the ordinary play of economic forces will
be modified or superseded by wider social considerations. In several nations this development
of public employment has gone so far that some
10 per cent. of the workers are thus removed from
the ordinary labour market. As this process
advances, its direct and indirect influences upon
the distribution of wealth will grow. If, along
with the increase of public employment, the public
enforcement of a minimum wage and other improvements in the conditions of labour, affecting
profits, take place, important effects upon the
growth and application of capital, as regards the
various industries and the various areas, may be
expected. We may even pass into an epoch of
' blackleg ' states which, refusing to conform to
the expensive standards imposed upon industry
in more advanced nations, suck an increasing
quantity of the savings of such nations, to be

applied within their areas to ' sweated industries.'
More and more will advanced political states be
confronted with the effects of the cosmopolitanism
of modern industry and the limitations thus set
upon their full control of the economic forces
operating inside their borders.

Closely related to this political consideration
is the new economic situation which may be set
up at no distant date by the industrialism of the
Far East and particularly of China, a country
containing some four hundred millions of population more nearly approaching the hypothetical
' economic man ' than any other people in the
world. Though certain recent observers are disposed to assign to China a slow pace of development in modern capitalistic industry, even a comparatively slow advance might exercise a quite
appreciable influence both upon the investment
market and the commerce of the world. If any
large proportion of this flood of cheap, fairly
efficient, and rapidly reproductive, labour were
made available, either by immigration or by
foreign trade, for competition in the labour
market of the world, it might offset the whole
of the influence of the declining birth-rate of the
Western peoples.

The immediate effect of the effective admission
of any large section of China into the world-

market would be to depress world-prices. This must follow from the fact that, China being a land of low prices from our Western standpoint, its admission would mean a far larger proportionate addition to the goods side of the equation of exchange than to the money side. Though prices in China would gradually rise to the general level, and a higher standard of consumption might correct the first effect, it seems reasonable to expect that the quick opening up of China might furnish an important correction to the prices acting at present to raise world-prices. But here again we should have to bear in mind the enormous new scope for investment involved in this developmental process, and the correspondingly large stimulation of credit, and therefore of the aggregate amount of money, which might attend the process.

The citation of these large unpredictable forces suffices to show the folly of attempting positively to forecast either the movement of prices or the remuneration of labour in the near or distant future.

The accelerating pace of internationalism, through trade, investments and migration of labour, is a factor of baffling significance. Statesmen and economists alike have been slow to recognize that the increasing domination of world markets for goods, capital and labour is rapidly encroaching upon the efficacy of purely national policies in all matters of vital economic and social import.   The determination of prices, and through prices of the material conditions of work and life, is more and more passing beyond the control of local or national groupings.   At present they are drifting into a more and more fortuitous condition, as regards most trade and most people. This tendency will bring increasing uncertainty and anxiety into the lives of men unless some organized endeavour to understand and to control these world-movements is set on foot.

A fuller, larger and more certain body of facts is the first requisite.   Large numbers of business men, politicians, publicists and economists are alive to the importance of a comprehensive inquiry into the nature, causes and effects of the recent rise of prices.   Many are willing and anxious to co-operate in such an inquiry.   But private co-operation alone will not suffice.   The governments of the different nations must agree to promote an investigation within their several borders conducted upon a common plan, in order to obtain the reliable measured facts required for the wide world-survey.   The carrying out of this project would furnish a fund of information relating to prices which, submitted to scientific digestion, might form the basis of a genuinely international policy. Whatever proposals might be made for the regulation of the output of gold, the adoption of an international clearing-house system, the establishment of a tabular standard of value, or any other device for monetary economy or stability of prices, would involve for their effective adoption an agreement of the governments of the leading industrial nations. As in point of fact, and as a matter of private enterprise, finance has attained a far more advanced degree of internationalism than any other human relation, it is reasonable to expect that the international government, which is slowly emerging, as a necessity from the growing tangle of extra-national relations between members of various countries, should first address itself to establishing orderly relations in world-markets and the values which they handle.

CHAPTER VIII

THE THEORY OF MONEY AND PRICES

§ I. THOUGH the main problem which has engaged our attention has been the practical one of seeking an explanation of the chief causes and effects of the phenomenon of rising prices, it is worth while considering what light our investigation sheds upon the theory of the monetary regulation of prices known as 'the quantity theory.'

Now there is a sense in which the so-called quantity theory is a simple self-evident proposition, to the effect that a price expresses the ratio between the quantity of money paid for goods and the quantity of goods sold.

That being so, every increase in the proportion of money to goods involves a correspondent rise of prices, every decrease a fall. This theory admits no question, and requires no exposition. It neither raises nor solves any problem. But in this self-evident statement 'money' means applied purchasing power of every kind, without regard to whether the instrument used is gold or silver coins, notes, cheques or anything else which sellers will accept in payment for goods. If in any given period of time the respective numbers of each of these various sorts of 'money' actually used in purchases were added up, were then multiplied by the average number of times each sort were used in payment (its velocity), and then the totals of each sort of money were added so as to form an aggregate, this aggregate would constitute the total quantity of money. Similarly the different kinds of goods, multiplied by the number of transactions in which they figured, would form the total quantity of goods.

It would then be true that the price level would vary directly and proportionately with every variation in the proportion of 'money' to 'goods.' For money would simply mean quantity of payment made on goods, while goods would mean quantity of goods supplied for payment. If twice as much money were paid this year as was paid last year for the same goods, prices would evidently have doubled ; if 25 per cent. less money were paid prices would have fallen a quarter. This is the meaning we have adopted for 'money' and for 'goods' in our setting of the equation of exchange. It is true we have not much concerned ourselves with the respective amounts of the different sorts of money and their respective rates of velocity, because this analysis appeared otiose. For practical purposes we preferred to take the aggregate of money as consisting of gross incomes, plus new gold coming into currency and new credit, disregarding the particular forms taken by the monetary instruments.

If money be thus taken as equivalent to aggregate of monetary payments during a given period, the 'quantity theory of money' is absolutely correct.

It can, however, hardly be called a theory: it is the simple exposition of an obvious fact.

§2. But in the controversy which takes place round 'the quantity theory' money is commonly not used in this clear comprehensive sense. As in Professor Fisher's recent exposition,[1] a distinction is often made between a narrower meaning of money and this full meaning, and a 'quantity theory' is erected on the basis of the narrower meaning. This narrower meaning virtually confines 'money' to legal tender, excluding the influence of deposit currency or cheques, on the ground that the latter forms of purchasing power are directly and closely controlled by the quantity of money in the narrower sense; and, finally, it

[1] *The Purchasing Power of Money.*

makes the quantity of gold the supreme determinant of price-movements.

It may be well to cite two passages from Professor Fisher's important work which bring out this crucial issue.   He breaks up the 'quantity theory' into five factors.   First comes Money in the narrower sense, coin and notes, 'actual money,'[1] and briefly designated M.   Next comes Deposits, against which cheques are drawable, designated M^1.   Each of these has its respective velocity, the average number of transactions in which it figures, known as V and V^1.   The fifth factor is volume of Trade, known as T, the equivalent of what we term Goods.

Now the first definition of the quantity theory [2] avowedly confines it to the narrower Money.
" The so-called ' quantity theory,' *i.e.* that prices vary proportionately to money, has often been incorrectly formulated, but (overlooking cheques) the theory is correct in the sense that the level of prices varies directly with the quantity of money in circulation, provided the velocity of circulation of that money and the volume of trade which it is obliged to perform are not changed."

This statement is in itself indisputable.   But regarded as a contribution to the explanation

[1] P. 45.   [2] P. 15.

of price-movement its worth depends upon (1) the validity of ' overlooking cheques,' and (2) the validity of assuming the unchanged character of velocity of circulation. Now in advanced communities the major part of the ' money ' which operates on prices consists of cheques. Can they be ' overlooked ' with any advantage ? Only upon one supposition, viz. that their quantity is directly governed by the quantity of legal tender, *i.e.* that M^1 varies directly and proportionately with M. Now this direct regulation of deposits by gold and notes, ultimately by gold, Professor Fisher appears to maintain. Indeed his whole case for the final dependence of price-movements upon quantity of gold is based upon this doctrine. Observe, however, the curiously qualified language in which the doctrine is affirmed. " It has even been argued that this interposition of circulating credit breaks whatever connexion there may be between prices and the quantity of money. This would be true if circulating credit were independent of money. But the fact is that the quantity of circulating credit, M^1, tends to hold a definite relation to M, the quantity of money in circulation ; that is, deposits are normally a more or less definite multiple of money." [1]   Observe that in the last

[1] P. 50.

sentence we have the relation between money and deposits first described as 'definite,' then as 'more or less definite,' with the further qualification of the term 'normally'!

A more formal statement of this relation appears as one of eight 'simple' propositions. "(8) There *tends* to be a *normal* ratio of bank deposits (M^1) to the quantity of money (M^1); because business convenience dictates that the available currency shall be apportioned between deposits and money in *a certain more or less definite, even though elastic, ratio.*" [1]

Now taking into consideration the 'tendency,' the 'normality,' the 'more or less definiteness' and the 'elasticity,' very little stiff substance remains in this proposition. Yet upon it hinges the whole of the theory that quantity of gold output is the sole ultimate regulator of prices, upon the money side of the equation of exchange.

If the proposition with all its qualifying language means no more than this, that since gold is one necessary ingredient in the manufacture of credit, *other things equal*, credit, and so money in the larger sense, will vary with the supply of gold, no exception need be taken to it, except that it bloats out into supreme prominence a factor the actual determinant value of which is

[1] P. 54. The italics are mine.—J. A. H.

10

greatly exceeded by several of the other things assumed as equal.

Now turn to the other qualification, the assumption that the velocity of circulation of M and M^1 is unchanged. Professor Fisher thinks this is warranted by affirming not that the velocity of circulation does in fact tend to remain unchanged, but that its changes are not governed or affected by the quantity of M or M^1. He recognizes that a number of forces are at work, increasing or decreasing the rate of circulation, but because they are independent of M or M^1 he feels justified in ignoring them in his statement of the quantity theory.

Now this is very curious. It is surely to be expected that in order to prove that quantity of gold normally rules prices, Professor Fisher would feel obliged to show that the aggregate of money in our sense of money payments was directly governed by the quantity of gold. In order to show this, it is necessary first to insist that deposits, or circulating credit, is governed by gold ; secondly, that the rates of circulation both of gold and of deposits or cheques are similarly governed. Now the first he does assert. But by denying the dependence of rate of circulation upon quantity of gold he greatly weakens, if he does not destroy, the efficacy of his quantity theory.

For what does it really come to ?

" Since, then, a doubling in the quantity of money (1) will normally double deposits subject to cheques in the same ratio [*sic*] and (2) will not appreciably affect either the velocity of circulation of money, or of deposits, or the volume of trade, it follows necessarily and mathematically that the level of prices must double." [1]   In other words, since quantity of money, in the sense of gold, is admittedly one factor in determining prices, if we exclude all other factors, prices will vary with money.   Surely a most attenuated doctrine! Similarly, if we took any other factor, as, for example, the extension of banking facilities, and excluded all other factors, a quantity theory could be erected on this basis.   " We may now restate, then, in what causal sense the quantity theory is true.   It is true in the sense that one of *the normal effects of an increase in the quantity of money is an exactly proportional increase in the general level of prices.*" [2]

It may, however, be said, that if gold does closely regulate deposits, or credit currency, and if it can be shown that whatever causes affect circulation are of independent origin, there is a reasonable presumption that an increase or decrease of gold will be accompanied by a rise or a fall of prices.   But, if causes affecting circulation, and

[1] P. 156.   [2] P. 157, the italics are Professor Fisher's.

therefore affecting the aggregate of purchasing power, are normally at work, as assuredly they are, it cannot be true that " the normal effect of an increase in the quantity of money is an exactly proportionate increase in the general level of prices." These 'normal effects' can only be presumed to occur when there are no disturbing forces, but if the disturbance is itself normal it destroys the normality of these effects.

No useful 'quantity theory' can be established in this way by eliminating other factors of importance that are normally co-operating with, or counteracting, quantity of money in the determination of prices.

§ 3. The same defective logic invalidates another recent exposition of the same 'quantity theory' by Sir David Barbour. " All prices and wages, therefore, could only rise in these islands above their present level, other things being equal, if there was a proportionate increase of gold in use as money, whether such money be used to meet casual and occasional payments or as reserves in the banks," [1] and again, " I have now shown that, other things being equal, prices cannot rise all round without a proportionate increase of money, and that if the supply of money be reduced, they must fall in proportion." [1]

[1] *The Standard of Value*, p. 40.

It is thus evident that the worth of the quantity theory in the form in which Professor Fisher and Sir David Barbour desire to apply it depends upon the relative validity or invalidity of their qualification, "*ceteris paribus.*"

Now there are two conditions under which propositions so qualified may be admitted as useful and true for scientific or for practical purposes.   One is that the 'other things' whose 'equality' is assumed are trifling in character, of the nature which is designated friction in mechanics, or 'personal equation' in the art of observation.   The other is that the other things are either known to be so contrary in disposition, or so numerous in independent origin, that there is a sound presumption that they will cancel out.   In either of these cases such a qualification may not impair the validity of a law.

But if the other things are important and do not tend to cancel out, they may destroy the entire value of the proposition.

Now this is actually the case with the 'other things' here treated as negligible.   For among them are such things as the expansion of banking facilities, the financial reconstruction of great industries so as to increase the proportion of wealth available as security for credit, and a development of profitable foreign investments on a scale of unprecedented magnitude and celerity. It is clearly in these regions of commerce and finance that we have the chief explanation of the enormous expansion of credit which has been upon the monetary side of the equation the principal cause of rising prices.

§ 4. But it is now time to return to the other fundamental assumption upon which Professor Fisher builds, viz. that credit varies directly and proportionately with gold, being in fact determined entirely by it. There is no ground whatever for this assumption. Admitting that gold plays some part in facilitating and checking the great recent growth of credit, no fixity of quantitative relation between the two amounts can be maintained. Gold is not a base upon which is reared a block of credit that enlarges and shrinks with the length of the base line. It is not a weight to which the weights of other monetary instruments must adjust themselves. It is not even an anchor securing the vessel of finance in times of storm. The real basis of credit is goods and the increase of actual credit is attributable to the increase of this goods-basis and the concomitant increase in demand for credit arising from the expansion of new large profitable business enterprises.

Even if it appears from monetary statistics, that in some particular country, as in the United

States, the growth of deposits during a certain period has kept tolerably close pace or proportion with the growth of gold funds, the controlling power of gold is by no means to be inferred. Having regard to the number and importance of other independent factors which admittedly enter in as determinants, such proportionateness of growth may reasonably be attributed to mere coincidence. Or, if it be argued that, since gold is by admission one necessary ingredient in the manufacture of credit, some proportion must subsist between the two, the main current of causation would be not from gold to credit, but from credit to gold. The pressure of demand for credit would be a far more potent factor in determining the supply of gold than would the supply of gold in determining the supply of credit. In point of fact, however, statistics of bank deposits show that in most countries [1] the rate of growth during the twenty years preceding 1895, when gold output was practically stationary, was quite as rapid as during the subsequent fifteen years. Moreover, so far as approximately reliable statistics are available, it is found that in different countries a very wide variation takes place in the rate of growth of gold and of deposits respectively. This is natural enough. Since the rates between

[1] Cf. Layton, *An Introduction to the Study of Prices*, pp. 136–8.

the two must be materially affected by every improvement in banking and financial machinery, as well as by the spread of knowledge and of confidence in the trading and investing sections of each population.

§ 5. What plausibility attaches to the quantity theory interpreted as a gold control rests upon a hidden acceptance of the assumption that every piece of money with which payment is made must either contain, or be able to procure, a quantity of gold of the same value as the goods which it helps to exchange. But this assumption rests in its turn upon a totally erroneous assumption as to what people want money for. If every one who receives a sovereign for a sack of wheat or a pair of shoes were going to consume that sovereign, as the other will consume the wheat or shoes, the assumption that the monetary form must be equal in value to the wheat or shoes would hold. But the recipient of the sovereign paid for wheat or shoes has no intention of consuming it : what he wants it for is to use it to get hold of something which he does want to consume. He wants this single service of transfer which it is able to render to him. A sovereign, then, in circulation must be regarded as a vehicle of transport, an instrument in the processes of commerce or exchange, which passes through the temporary possession of a series of persons, each of whom receives it and uses it for this single act of service.

Since this single act of service is all they want to get from it, they must not rightly be regarded as the owners of the sovereign, in the sense in which they own either their consumable goods or their capital instruments, but as the hirers of the pieces of money which thus pass into and through their hands. Accept this standpoint and it becomes apparent that the real price of money which concerns us is not the market-price of goods, but the hire-price paid to owners of money for the use of money. Now what do we mean by the owners of money? We have just said that the ordinary tradesman who receives money in payment for goods is not rightly regarded as owner, but only as temporary occupier of the money. But there are people who own money, using it as a permanent possession, and letting it out to other people who only want a temporary use of it. These people are bankers. They are the only people who are large owners of money, whose business capital consists chiefly of money. The real price of money is the price paid to these persons for the use of money. In other words, it is the hire-price not the purchase-price that is the real ' price of money.' The distinctively financial use of ' price of money ' is the true use.

This point of view alone affords an escape from what is otherwise a hopeless impasse, or paradox, viz. the apparent divergence in the movement of the hire-price and the purchase-price of money. In the case of all other things which are subjects alike for sale and hire, such as land, houses, motor cars, furniture, the hire-prices and the purchase-prices always vary together, though not always at precisely the same pace. It would be impossible to conceive the general price for houses to be rising over a period of years while the rents of these houses were falling. If motor cars become cheaper to buy, we know they will become cheaper to hire. We understand well the necessity of the agreement in the movement of the two sets of prices. What is the price of such a thing but the capitalized value of its rental? Uncertainty as to the future events, which may affect the utility or saleable value of any of these forms of property, may, indeed, affect the relation between the sale and the hire price, *e.g.* the number of years' purchase constituting the capital value of a house may increase or diminish. So the capital value and sale-price of certain classes of house property have shrunk in recent years considerably more than the annual rental of these same properties. But this is attributable to special and abnormal causes affecting the calculability of the future value of such goods, in view of the modern mobility of population and industry on the one hand, and swift transformations in means of transit on the other. In other words, buying a house may involve new elements of risk which hiring a house escapes. So the hire-price and the purchase-price may to some extent diverge. But no such explanation is applicable to money. Why should the quantity of goods which I can get for lending £100 be as great or greater than it was ten years ago, while the quantity I can get for selling £100 is so much less ? What is the meaning of this apparently large divergence between the hire-price and the purchase-price of money ? [1]

[1] It will be convenient here to point out that part of the rise in hire-price, rate of interest, may not unreasonably be considered a result of a continuous upward movement of prices. So far as lenders look far ahead, they will require for permanent or long loans, such as investments in Government stock or railway debentures, a higher rate of interest if they believe that prices will continue to move upward. For in a continuous rise of prices the fixed money interest from their investment will command a smaller quantity of real wealth. Under such circumstances the capital value of their investment will also be shrinking. A higher rate of interest will be required under such circumstances to yield the same real remuneration for saving than in a period of falling or stable prices. How far this actually has operated to raise the rate of interest since the rise of prices began it is impossible to say, but some part must be accredited to it.

The only satisfactory answer I can find is that the so-called purchase-price of money is not a true price at all, that the commonly adopted economic view, to the effect that money is bought and sold and passes in exchange on equal terms with ordinary commodities, is erroneous. It is always the hire-price of money that really counts on a parity with other prices. Money is in reality always hired and never bought outright except by a few classes of persons who are ' money dealers.'

§ 6. Once accept this view, the primary importance of the hire-price of this money is evident. The person who receives a sum of money for goods he has sold, holding it in his possession until the second part of the exchange transaction takes place, by which he parts with this money in payment for the goods he wants for his own use, is not, save in a purely formal and legal way, the owner of the money which he temporarily holds. He does not regard it as his property in the same sense as he regards the goods he holds for sale or for consumption, or the plant or other capital which earns him his income. It is for him only a passing instrument in the commercial process. He values it simply from this instrumental standpoint. The fact that token coins and inconvertible notes will under certain circumstances perform all the functions of the best money, proves that equality of commercial values between the substance figuring as money and the goods it buys is not essential. Modern money is becoming essentially ' token ' in its character. This truth is not impaired by the fact that sometimes ' token ' money fails, and, through fear lest it should not carry to completion the process of exchange of goods, the exchange instrument is found to resume its primitive condition of equal utility with the goods whose exchange it is to bring about.

The attitude of the ordinary business man towards money is that of a man hiring a vehicle for a single journey, not that of a man buying a vehicle for continuous service. Perhaps a nearer analogy [1] is that of the man who buys soda water in siphons, paying the full price of each siphon when he buys the soda water, but getting it back again when he wants more. If one supposes that he can return standard siphons at any shop where he happens to deal, the analogy becomes closer. Under such circumstances the

[1] None of these analogies is exact. If monetary forms are ' vehicles ' they are expansible and contractible vehicles whose power of conveyance fluctuates with their number, the element of truth in ' the quantity theory.' If they are bottles they carry sometimes more and sometimes less. This limitation of the analogies does not, however, invalidate them for the purpose to which they are here applied.

deposit he paid for siphons might be kept at a considerably greater amount than the actual market-price for siphons, as indeed is commonly the case. The fact, that the siphons standing empty in his cellar are not worth the money he has paid for them, does not trouble him. He will get it all back. These siphons are ' tokens ' to the extent to which the deposit on them differs from their market value. But for the ordinary man the market value of siphons has no concern, it is only this hire-price of them that matters for him. The bottle manufacturer and the soda water manufacturer alone are concerned with the intrinsic value of the siphons.

So the gold-miner, the bullion merchant and the banker are concerned with the intrinsic value of sovereigns and other monetary instruments. The concern of ordinary persons is to hire these instruments and to get from each of them that comes into their hand the single use which they require from it.

§ 7. A provisional acceptance of this standpoint has the merit of a hypothesis that fits the facts and ' explains ' our paradox of the rising hire-price and the falling purchase-price of ' money.' If money has not really a sale-price at all (except for bankers and financiers) but only a hire-price, the general rise of prices assumes a different economic character from that usually accorded to it. It becomes a secondary result of the main factor in the modern financial solution, the rapid expansion of that money-hiring which we call credit.

We then get the following order of events. A concurrence of a rapid development of the system for supplying credit on hire, with a similarly rapid development of opportunities for making profitable use of credit (*i.e.* an expansion of supply and demand for credit), has brought into the world-markets an enormous volume of credit. The demand for this credit has kept full pace with the supply, tending to exceed it, so that the hire-price has risen.

The actual increase of money mainly consists of an expanding volume of credit, based primarily upon goods and hired out to business men. It is this volume of hired money that accounts for the acceleration of the supply of money which in the various markets confronts the retarded supply of goods, and so, in accordance with the only view of the quantity theory that has any meaning, automatically raises prices. The fact, that such a rise of prices should occur, no-wise impairs the view just presented that money to the ordinary business man is 'token' rather than of intrinsic value. Any swelling of the value of admittedly token coins or inconvertible notes notoriously operates to raise prices. The rise of prices that has taken place, therefore, is due directly to the increased quantity of money in proportion to goods. But that increased quantity of money is itself primarily due to the increased supply and demand for credit or hired token money, not to the rush of gold or to the merely mechanical building up of credit on an enlarged gold-base.

§ 8. In such an exposition there remains, however, a point of great doubt and difficulty. Our view of money in circulation is that it is hired, not owned. If that be so, it would appear that every one who gets a use of money, in order to effect an exchange, must pay a hire-price for this single use, just as every one who gets the use of the postal system to convey news, or of a railway truck to convey coal, must pay for a service that involves an economic cost. Now how this hire-price is paid in the case of money owned by governmental or other bankers, and lent by way of loan on discount to borrowers who want it for a single act of purchase, is evident. In the case of a discounted bill the discounting-house takes the hire-price in advance, paying for the bill a sum of money slightly less than the sum which the bill purports to represent and which will be paid to meet it when it falls due. Part of this deduction is for risk, but part is a true hire-price for the single use made by the money advanced in order to enable the recipient to effect a purchase. He has sold some goods of his own, receives in payment a bill, gets that bill discounted by a banker or broker, and with the bank money thus obtained buys the goods of some one else which he requires for his own use or consumption. Two parties have presumably been benefited by this discount operation, A. who bought B.'s goods, paying by means of a bill instead of by cash which he had not got, and B., who by means of this discounted bill was able to exchange the goods he had to sell for the goods he wanted to buy more quickly or on better terms. Since A. and B. have each made an economic gain by the discount operation, it is fair to assume that each of them has paid something to the banker for the service rendered. Though in the face of it B. has paid the whole in the shape of the discount, it is reasonable to assume that A. has not got his gain for nothing, but has paid his share of the price for the instrument of exchange. Nor is it difficult to see how he has paid it. If he had paid cash to B. for the goods, instead of accepting a bill, that cash payment would

11

have been a little smaller than the sum for
which the bill is drawn.   The larger sum which
A. will have to pay to the holder of the bill, when
he ' meets ' it at maturity, will contain his contribution to the hire-price of the credit form.
The significance of this case lies in the example
it affords of the payment of a hire-price concealed
in the use of a document purporting to be a sale-
price of goods.   A. pays a hire-price for a credit
instrument that is open and obvious.   But B. has
also paid a hire-price wrapped up in the so-called
sale-price for the goods he buys.

We have here taken the case of a bill which
enables A. to sell his goods to B. and buy some
other goods, performing the function of money
in transacting a single exchange of goods for
goods, and getting a hire-price, actually paid by
the two parties, but formally paid by him who
has the bill discounted.   But a bill once brought
into commercial existence may, during the period
of its life, have some further currency, passing
through several hands, and so performing the
function of money several times before it is
ultimately cancelled.   In that case we must
suppose that each of the parties that gets a
use of exchange out of it must make some payment for that use, contributing a bit towards
the total hire-price paid either to the banker or

broker who has discounted it, or to the person in whose favour the bill is drawn, in case the bill circulates as purchasing power without being discounted. If it be agreed that each party getting a use of exchange must make some contribution towards the hire-price of the instrument, there is only one way in which that contribution can be made, so far as the parties whose names are not originally involved in the discounted bill are concerned. Now the use each of them gets out of the money is in the act of purchase it enables them to perform. Their contribution then, if made at all, must be made by means of a slight raising of the price of the goods they buy with the bill. This raising of price, regarded from the standpoint of the seller, represents the lower value he sets upon the bill as compared with a payment in legal tender: it represents the lower degree of its security or availability as purchasing power.

What applies to a bill also applies in various degrees to other forms of credit-notes with which purchasing is done. All such instruments, from bank-notes or cheques to promissory-notes, so far as they circulate or pass in currency, are re-discounted each time they pass, in terms of the price of the goods they buy. In this way each person who gets a use of such an instrument as purchasing power pays his hire-price for that use. Every credit instrument received in payment tends to raise the price of the goods it buys, so as to compensate the buyer for any risk or defect of acceptability which belongs to it. The loss represented by this enhancement of price is the hire-price paid by the user of the credit instrument for the single service that it renders him.

That service consists in enabling him to make a purchase which otherwise he could not have made, or made so soon. The performance of this service involves using a monetary instrument whose production and operation is attended with some cost to the issuer. This cost consists partly in losing the current use of the cash kept as guarantee against the failure of the drawer of the bill to meet it, partly in the risk of losing the whole amount advanced. Towards this cost each user of the bill or note makes his contribution.

So far as bankers are engaged in making loans or advances, it thus appears that the hire price for the credit money which they manufacture out of the concrete wealth tendered as security and the capital (including gold reserve) which they own, is paid by those who use the credit. The same evidently applies to the other monetary services which bankers by their deposit and cheque system render to their customers. The greater security and velocity given to coins and other monetary forms of legal tender by the bank deposit and cheque system enables every holder of money to get a better use out of it than he could by keeping it in his till, quite apart from the fact that the banker will pay him a part of the hire-price he makes for loaning the greater part of his deposits. The payment customers make to bankers on current accounts may be regarded as a price for using a more mobile form of money instead of a less mobile.

Every credit instrument is kept in currency on condition that such a payment is made each time it is used. The effect of an increasing utilization of such forms of credit money will be to raise general prices, by enhancing the aggregate of purchasing power, and weighting a larger proportion of costs of purchase with this hire-cost of the money used in payment.

§ 9. But what of the gold and other legal tender issued by governments? Does each person who uses a sovereign or a £5 note of the Bank of England pay a price for its use? This of course need not occur. A Government could provide a 'free' currency, just as it could provide a 'free' postal system, by charging the whole expense upon the revenue raised by taxes. It does not do this with the postal system, but charges each user a hire-price for the use of its postal machinery on the occasion of each service rendered.

One form of purchasing power issued by Government, viz. postal money orders, is evidently paid for upon terms which include a hire-price. At the time you buy the stuff, you pay something for the use of the bottle. You do not, however, appear to pay in this way for the use of coins issued from the Mint or notes issued by the Bank of England.

The Government buys gold from bullion merchants, makes it into coins, or manufactures paper substitutes, and puts these coins and notes into current use. These money instruments thus cost the Government something to make and to keep in repair. The Government must hand over to the bullion merchants, mine owners, etc., nearly the whole of the coins made out of the gold they buy from them, or notes based on that gold, or some other form of general purchasing power which, properly interpreted, means a general command over the wealth of the nation.

This order upon the general wealth means a right vested in these bullion merchants, miners, etc., to demand a portion of the general body of commodities, services and new forms of capital, in payment for furnishing materials for manufacturing legal tender. Had these materials of the new supply of Government money been withheld, and so this increased demand for general wealth not been created, the total purchasing power of the community would have been so much less. Moreover, if the capital and labour expended in gold mines upon the production of this gold had been employed in other industries, a larger aggregate of goods would have been produced. But a smaller aggregate amount of purchasing power, applied to buy a larger quantity of goods, would have meant a lower range of prices.[1] Thus, the effect of the Government payment of the costs of manufacturing and issuing new legal tender is to raise prices.

This general rise of prices is the direct result of the payment made by the Government for the gold. For when the gold merchants, etc., apply this payment in demand for goods, or services, or securities, they raise the prices of what they buy. In fact, this is the only method (barring taxation) by which the deduction of the real wealth, required to pay the producers of gold, can be made. If Government buys gold to make

---

[1] This statement, however, needs some qualification. In so far as the increased output of money facilitates commerce and industry, not merely raising prices, it assists to produce a larger quantity of goods. This increased quantity of goods is a partial offset against the increased quantity of money, and mitigates its influence in raising prices.

a million more sovereigns, paying the bullion merchants £980,000 for the gold, the real wealth into which these gold merchants convert their money is taken by a series of minute deductions from the real wealth of the rest of the community. These deductions are made in the shape of a slight enhancement of all prices, or, in other words, by a slight reduction in the amount of real wealth which everybody gets by spending a sovereign.   It may here be remarked that it is not only the particular persons who make use of the new sovereigns thus coined who pay this hire-price.   Since that price is exacted through a general rise of price, everybody using any form of money contributes his share.   But that fact does not impair the validity of this method of interpreting what takes place.   If we take the process of the governmental supply of currency as a whole, all members of the community use this currency and pay for its use in the manner I describe, by means of a slight sacrifice of the real wealth which they would have enjoyed, had it not been deemed socially desirable thus to create a currency.

It matters nothing, however, to the substance of this explanation whether the payment for this use of money is regarded as a hire-price paid by each person, or as an indirect process of taxation incurred by a commercial community for the supply of the legal currency it requires.

§ 10. Two conclusions may be drawn. The Government or Government Bank is and remains the sole owner of the legal tender it issues. Though a legal ownership is vested in the person who in the process of its circulation happens to be its momentary holder, this does not express the economic substance of the case. Government lets out this money for the performance of a series of financial operations, each of which is paid for by the person who gets the use of the operation. This continued ownership by the Government has even its legal recognition in the laws prohibiting clipping or defacement, and in the power to ' call in ' its money when it desires to do so.

Once realize consistently that bankers and governments are the only bodies that require to own and keep possession of money,[1] and that all that private citizens or business men require is the passing services of particular pieces of money as instruments enabling them to exchange the

---

[1] This needs a slight qualification. Though bankers and financiers are the only business men whose capital consists predominantly in the possession of money, every business requires to have a small quantity of till-money. In a modern organized business, however, that is almost a negligible factor.

goods they want to sell for those they want to buy, several difficulties are cleared up. It then becomes intelligible that, at ordinary times and in ordinary circumstances, they need not and will not insist upon the intrinsic value of the money instruments, but only upon their efficiency to do the work required of them. This work at most times has been partly done by money instruments which do not even pretend to an economic value equivalent to that of the goods whose exchange they effect. Token coins and inconvertible notes of insignificant intrinsic value can perform the function of stable money, if their supply is honestly regulated. Indeed our great monetary system of bank money in the shape of notes and cheques does not really stand upon the steady basis of a right to demand and receive gold which their forms profess. For it is well known that a large part of the notes have no gold behind them in the coffers of the Bank, and that the gold reserve which is supposed to support the general liabilities of bankers would be quite inadequate to meet a financial crisis. More and more in modern civilized countries financial crises are met by a suspension of the right to demand the gold which notes and cheques profess to give, and the substitution of some governmental or banker's certificate which relies for its worth in the last resort upon the fact that people will accept it as payment for goods. This means that goods, not gold, are the basis of the modern money system. Once grasp this principle, and it becomes intelligible why gold itself when used as money is sinking from its old character of intrinsic value and becoming a form of token money. More and more, persons receiving gold in payment are ceasing to ask whether the intrinsic value of this gold is equivalent to that of the goods they have sold for it, or those they wish to buy with it. They know that the power to sell and to buy which the coin possesses does not any longer closely depend upon the amount of its inherent value. They recognize it as a passing instrument of exchange, like a note, cheque or token coin, which Government and bankers own but ordinary men hire for single uses. If this view be correct, it explains how the so-called rise of prices or depreciation of gold may occur at a time when the rate of discount which constitutes its hire-price has risen. The depreciation is an expression of the tendency of people to treat gold in the light of token money. Of course that tendency has not yet gone very far. There are many communities, and some classes in every community, that have some fairly close regard to the intrinsic value of gold. For stable international relations some sufficient gold reserve, as we have already intimated, may long continue to be necessary.

But, just in proportion as the token or merely instrumental value of gold gains upon its intrinsic value in the minds of ordinary users, will it be possible for a depreciation of gold to take place, at a time when the rise of its hire-price shows that there is no excess of supply of gold. It must be added that this change in the attitude of individuals towards gold, regarding it more in the light of token money, would not, of course, in itself bring about its depreciation or a rise of general prices. That rise of prices, as we have consistently maintained, can only be directly attributed to an increase in the proportion of purchasing power to goods. The causes of that increase in proportion of money have been traced. The increase of gold supply has been recognized as one, though not a principal efficient cause. When an enlargement of the supply of money as compared with goods has been brought about, prices rise, quite irrespective of the cost of producing the various sorts of monetary instruments.

Because so large an increase of the supply of acceptable money has been made, all sorts of that money, including the gold coins, suffer a depreciation of purchasing power. There is no reason why the depreciation, or rise of prices, should not continue until the purchase-price of an ounce of gold coined into money diverged a good deal further from the hire-price of the same gold. But so long as gold is to any considerable extent needed as a material for the manufacture or support of money, that divergence between its purchase-price and its hire-price must have its limit. If a man in possession of an ounce of gold finds its hire-price rising and its purchase-price falling, he will be more and more disposed to loan his gold instead of selling it, *i.e.* instead of buying goods with it. In other words, he will be disposed to save a larger proportion of his money than before, and to spend a smaller. This will apply, of course, not only to the possession of gold, but to the possession of any sort of money. Saving will increase and spending decrease. This will tend to adjust the balance, reducing discount and interest, and reducing prices. The fact that the hire - price and the purchase-price of money have diverged is only intelligible upon the hypothesis that the recent conditions of the economic world required and evoked an increased proportion of saving. A larger proportion of the aggregate money incomes has been thus applied to the creation of credit, but the demand for credit, based upon the growing productivity of new capital, has grown even faster than the supply, raising somewhat the price. A result of the application of this increased saving and diminished spending has been to expand the volume of purchasing power at a faster pace than the volume of purchasable goods, and so to produce a rise of prices.

The rise of price is thus to be regarded as a secondary and incidental effect of the increased demand and supply of credit. Once accept the view that the money with which persons buy goods is not (save by a legal fiction) their own property, but consists of instruments of exchange, hired by them from a government, or bank, or other financial business, for the single use to which they are put, the paradox of rising hire-price and falling purchase-price becomes intelligible. The latter is unreal. Goods are not exchanged against gold, in the same sense in which coal is exchanged against cotton or corn. The latter sorts of exchange are the substance of all commerce, which always and exclusively consists in exchanging one sort of goods for another sort. No one, except for uses in the industrial arts, wants to exchange goods for gold, for no one wants the gold except as a passing instrument for obtaining other goods. This being so, no one will scrutinize the value of the instrument, except as regards its efficacy for the purpose in hand. So it becomes possible for a money instrument, whether coin or note, to have an instrumental or token value that is greater or less than the value which it would have, if it were regarded not as a hired instrument, but as a commodity held for consumption or for fixed use as capital. An instrument, which everybody hires for a brief use and no one wants to own, cannot be said to have a true sale-price, for there is no genuine market. The deposit on siphons or bottles may exceed or fall below the true cost of production and trade price within considerable limits. So with the quantity of goods handed over to secure the use of a money instrument. Provided the person is sure of being able to get the proper quantity of the goods he wants to get when he wants them, the temporary deposit on the vehicle does not much trouble him. Of course if there is any real doubt about the complete efficacy of the exchange implement, the case will be different. He will not hand over so much of his goods for money, unless he has confidence that this money will enable him to get so much of the other goods which he wants. And there may be times and circumstances when this confidence can only be obtained by insisting that the money instrument shall have a permanent intrinsic value equal to that of the goods he parts with and those he wants in exchange. If the purchaser of soda water had reason to fear that he might not be able to get his deposit back, or the whole of it, when he returned the siphons, he would consider closely the utility of siphons as a form of property, how much permanent use he could get out of them, or how much he could get for them in the open market. He would not consent to pay a deposit larger than that intrinsic value.

So it is with the person who ' deposits ' goods for gold or for any other money. If there is a doubt as to the full efficacy of that money for the particular exchange use for which he wants it, he will then look behind the hire-price to the purchase-price of the money. In a financial crisis, when this want of confidence in the ability of money to perform the operation for which it has been hired was widespread, people generally would take this view. They would then only consent to ' deposit ' or sell their goods for a quantity and sort of money which had a permanent commodity value equal to that of the goods. This abnormal attitude might, of course, have as its necessary consequence such a fall of prices as was needed to equalize the commodity value of an ounce of gold with that of the goods whose exchange it was required to effect. It not only might have, but it must have this effect, if there were a strict adherence to the right to demand gold as a sole legal tender. Indeed, for purposes of international commerce the present position of gold is such that a financial crisis of any broad character must for a time put general prices upon this basis. So far as a financial collapse of narrower or purely national area is concerned, the growing habit of accepting the guarantee of government or clearing-house paper as a sufficient support for the purchasing power of money is displacing the former tendency in crises to rush for gold in order to hold it as the sole security for the performance of the work of exchange. I do not contend that no other explanation is possible for the divergence between the hire-price (discount) and the purchase-price of money. But I suggest that the best explanation is afforded by considering the exceptional nature of the relation of the ordinary business man towards the instruments of exchange. He hires the use of them, but the conditions of his hiring are such as to place him in temporary legal ownership of the instruments he wants to use. But normally his attitude towards them is

12

that towards hired tools, the hire-price and not the sale-price of which is his concern.

I think that the full acceptance and application of this principle that money is only ' owned ' by governments, banks, and other financial firms, and is let out by them on various terms to those who want its temporary use, will clear up a good many obscurities in the movements of money and of prices.

INDEX

T - #0049 - 160425 - C0 - 198/129/11 [13] - CB - 9780415589406 - Gloss Lamination